CLASH OF WORLDS

Clash of Worlds

DAVID BURNETT

MARC

Eastbourne

Front cover photo: Zefa Picture Library

British Library Cataloguing in Publication Data

Burnett, David *1943–*
    Clash of worlds.
    1. Ideologies
    I. Title
    290

    ISBN 1–85424–107–9

Printed in Great Britain for
MARC, an imprint of Monarch Publications Ltd,
1 St Anne's Road, Eastbourne, E Sussex BN21 3UN by
Courier International Ltd, Tiptree, Essex
Typeset by Watermark, Norfolk House, Cromer

CONTENTS

FOREWORD

David Burnett's book is concerned throughout with just one subject – worldviews. Most of us have heard the word. Few of us know what it means. Here is the answer. I am not aware of any other book which deals so concisely and elegantly with the subject.

Clash of Worlds is beautifully written, illustrated with a multitude of anecdotes, revealing a profound scholarship as well as the great virtue of keeping tenaciously to the subject.

The particular worldviews of Hinduism and Islam, amongst others, are clearly set out. There is a sane, balanced assessment of the New Age movement. And the book works carefully through its own agenda: an understanding of contemporary worldviews, an understanding of our own worldview, an appreciation of the process of interaction between worldviews, and the development of principles for communicating with people of different worldview.

This is a book for people who are prepared to think. And it won't give you an unnecessary headache while you do it!

Peter Cotterell
Principal, London Bible College

PART I
Inner Worlds

1

OTHER WORLDS

'Now was the opportunity,' I thought, as I sat in the school classroom. The teacher had finally opened up a general discussion time with the class to discuss various philosophical ideas. I lifted my hand to raise the question which had puzzled me for some time. Taking a deep breath, I asked, 'How do I know that the world around me is actually real?' The look on the teacher's face and the tittering of the other students showed me that I had not been understood, so I repeated my question. 'How do I know that the world is really there and is not merely a projection in my own mind, like some film, which will one day come to an end?' The class erupted into laughter. The teacher politely said that the world is there because all our senses confirm the fact, and then moved on to another topic.

This particular incident has always remained in my mind because I knew that I was asking a question about something beyond normal topics of conversation. I was conscious of querying something which was taken to be an essential fact by my Western society. Here was some fundamental assumption which was considered beyond doubt, and yet at the same time it remained beyond proof.

Years later, I journeyed to the great land of India and there met with a Hindu guru sitting lotus-style dressed in a simple cloth. When I asked him my question he smiled knowingly, and acknowledged the insight behind my words. Why did the guru have such a different response to my question? As I began to understand the complexities of Indian culture, I began to comprehend the major differences in the assumptions which exist

11

between the West and the East. These differences have in recent years been called 'worldview', by behavioural scientists. I began to comprehend how important this concept was not just in understanding the ways of thinking of another people, but in grasping the assumptions of my own culture and my own Christian beliefs.

'Worldview' is to be the main topic of this book, and although we will seek to define and analyse its many aspects, there will always be an element of the indefinable. Worldview is not some objective reality, but something which formulates my perspective of what is real. Worldview has been defined in many ways. 'The central set of concepts and presuppositions that provide people with their basic assumptions about reality,' Whiteman.[1] 'A worldview is a set of presuppositions (or assumptions) which we hold (consciously or subconsciously) about the basic make-up of our world,' Sire.[2] To understand the significance of this concept of 'worldview' one must examine the implications of these definitions. What is a worldview?

A system of ideas and values

First, it is necessary to see the difference between worldview and culture in general. When we first venture to another culture we are initially impressed by the many and varied activities and objects. People dress in ways different to that of the visitor. They may live in houses of a different design, and eat what seem strange foods in exotic ways. Some people prefer to sit on the floor whilst others sit on chairs. Some greet one another by shaking hands, whilst others give a low bow or embrace each other. The new society seems to follow a profusion of customs and activities different to that familiar to the newcomer.

Anthropologists have shown that cultures are not merely random sets of strange customs and activities. Within each and every culture there is a system of order shared by all the members of that society. In this way, culture may be likened to a game of chess. To a person who has no knowledge of the game the players seem at first to be moving the strangely shaped pieces at random. With time the observer begins to see that there is an order and pattern for every piece, and then finally he begins to see that there is an overall strategy employed by the players. Culture may be likened to the game itself, whilst the worldview is the unseen set of rules which determines how the game can be played.

A worldview consists of the shared framework of ideas held by a particular society concerning how they perceive the world. Everyday experiences are fitted into this framework in order to give a totality of meaning and comprehension for the individual. To use a different analogy, culture may be likened to a tree in full leaf. When one looks at the tree, what is observed is a multitude of leaves. These may be regarded as being analogous

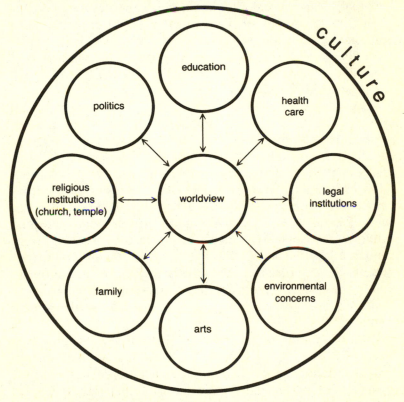

Figure 1.1 Interrelationship of worldview and culture

to the outward aspects of the culture which initially catch the interest of the visitor. More careful study shows that the shape and form of the tree does not depend upon the leaves, but the trunk and branches which are often lost amidst all the foliage. Similarly, the worldview gives shape and order to the multitude of outward manifestations of a culture (see Figure 1.1). Worldviews are made visible in the everyday living adopted by a person and his society.

Worldview is closely connected with theologies and philosophies, but it is much more than these. Theologies are organised systems of thought formulated by intellectuals to describe some ideal model of man's relationship with God. The term 'worldview', on the other hand, relates to ways of perceiving reality, and in so doing provides a deeper level of assumption than philosophy or theology. Philosophy is restricted to the intellectuals, but everyone has a worldview. By studying worldview, we are not merely looking at the religious beliefs of a society, though we will continually see the marked influence of religions on worldviews.

Louis J. Luzbetak has used the analogy of a living organism which again helps to differentiate between worldview and culture, 'An organism is more than its functioning parts; it has, in addition, a principle of life. Culture is likewise more than its functionally organized parts; it too has a "soul" that gives direction to its functions.'[3] Ruth Benedict borrowed terms from psychology, and spoke of Navaho culture as a typical introverted system: individualistic, self-centred, non-conformist and aggressive. The neighbouring Pueblo Indians were described by her as 'Apollonian', that is, highly group-conscious. Benedict argued that all behaviour within a culture will follow the pattern characteristic of the 'soul' of the particular culture.[4] Thus worldview can also be seen as the 'soul' of a given culture.

A more useful model than the single theme proposed by Benedict is that suggested by Opler and others.[5] Cultures are considered not to have one, but several closely related 'themes' which give direction and integration. A theme may be defined as an idea, or value which controls behaviour, and is generally approved by a society. It is these themes and ideas which we wish to explore and see how their interaction in the world today is causing many to question principles long held.

A set of assumptions

A second characteristic of worldview is that the ideas and values which it embraces always seem logical and obvious to the people of the particular culture. The worldview themes appear to be beyond dispute, and this is what caused the amusement of the school-children hearing the question about the reality of the material world. Their worldview is assumed as the obvious interpretation of how the world is ordered. Worldview consists of ideas which give comprehension and sense to the people who participate within that culture. As Robert Redfield has said: 'If "Culture" suggests the way a people look to an anthropologist, "worldview" suggests how everything looks to a people.... It is the way we see ourselves in relation to all else.'[6]

Jean La Fontaine tells the interesting incident of an anthropologist having a discussion on the Yap islands with a group of islanders who believed that the cause of conception is not sexual intercourse, but the entry of a spirit into the woman concerned. The anthropologist cited the example of the improvement in the quality of the pigs which had resulted from the cross breeding of imported European boars with native sows. The islanders were quite prepared to agree with this yet refused to accept the idea that sexual relations amongst humans resulted in pregnancy, citing various cases of married women without children, and ugly women, whom no man found attractive, having babies. The discussion caused puzzlement on both sides, until light dawned on a particular islander. 'Ah,' he said to his companions, 'this man actually believes that people are the same as pigs'. The end product of the discussion was not merely a greater understanding of the other culture, but of the beliefs of the participants in the dialogue.[7]

Anthropologists often say that people of different cultures

live in different worlds. This idea is based on the work of Edward Sapir in studying languages. He argued that 'the worlds in which different societies live are distinct worlds, not merely the same world with different labels attached.'[8] He asserts that the world one lives in depends on culture and the assumptions accepted by that particular culture. Some things seem incredulous from the viewpoint of one culture whilst acceptable to another.

Peter Wagner tells the story about the King of Siam who in the seventeenth century was pleased to talk to the Dutch ambassador.[9] He was enthralled by the stories of life in far-off Holland – that is until the ambassador began to tell the king about winter in Holland, and how the water could turn so hard that an elephant could walk on it. This was simply too much for the king who had lived his whole life in the tropics. The king replied, 'Hitherto I have believed the strange things you have told me, because I look upon you as a sober faithful man; but now I am sure you lie.' The king's worldview would not allow him to accept this idea.

A model to explain reality

A third characteristic of worldview is that it attempts to show order and predictability within everyday experiences. New facts or experiences are required to fit into the framework of ideas in order to make a unified system, and if not they are discarded. This is a way of making 'common-sense' of human experience. This can be shown by looking at an illusion as shown in Figure 1.2. What do you see? Is it a vase or two people's faces in profile? At one moment you may be admiring the contours of a symmetrical vase, and the next you see the profiles of two human heads facing one another. Experiments have demonstrated that the flipping back and forth of the image has nothing to do with the visual signals themselves. What seems to happen is that the mind is confronting a pattern that can be interpreted in at least two equally probable ways, and keeps jumping between each interpretation, testing various

Figure 1.2

hypotheses in an attempt to resolve the ambiguity. Ordinary life cannot be lived in a continual state of ambiguity, so one must accept one or the other perspective. Worldview enables a particular society and member of that society to make sense of the experiences in the world about them.

Hiebert pictures the relationship between external reality and the perception of that reality inside our heads in the form

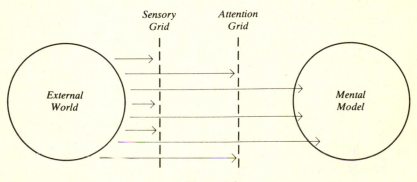

Figure 1.3

of the diagram shown in Figure 1.3.[10] The individual is bombarded by an immense amount of potential experiences, only a proportion of which the individual is able to interpret. Human hearing, for example, is only able to detect a limited band of all the vibrations which may be in the air. This is the principle behind the dog whistle which is inaudible to the owner, but clearly audible to the dog. The sun emits a whole spectrum of electromagnetic radiation, but only a small amount of that spectrum can be detected by the human eye.

Of all the experiences which an individual actually senses, many do not reach the level of the person's attention. Which parent has not known the frustration of speaking to their child who is engrossed in a television programme? Although one could be excused for assuming that their child had suddenly gone deaf, the fact is that the child is screening out all incidental experiences in their concentration on a limited number of experiences – the television.

Likewise, people from one culture may seem 'blind' to some experiences which seem obvious to people from another culture. This is because they are focusing their attention upon different things. Many language students have known the frustration of trying to copy the words spoken by their language helper. They repeat the words as carefully as they can so that to them it sounds exactly like the utterances of the teacher. But the teacher quickly moves to correct them, and repeats the words again. The poor student is left struggling to comprehend what to him is the incomprehensible differences between his sounds and those of the teacher. Only with time does the student begin to pick up the slight differences which are so important as far as the speaker of the language is concerned.

Hiebert argues that from perceived experiences, the individual attempts to form these into an organised mental model. Let us take a simple example of a model made up of dots and lines. Suppose the nine dots in Figure 1.4 represent bare facts and the lines represent the interpretive framework. It is obvious that the lines can be drawn in many different ways, and each one provides a particular interpretation of the dots. So it is with worldviews. One worldview may draw the lines of meaning between facts in one way and another worldview will draw the lines in a different way.

These recurrent models of reality have been called 'paradigms' (from the Greek *paradigma*, 'pattern') by some writers.[11] The term 'paradigm' is generally used as a label for some specific model, whilst 'worldview' is a term which is used

What do you see?

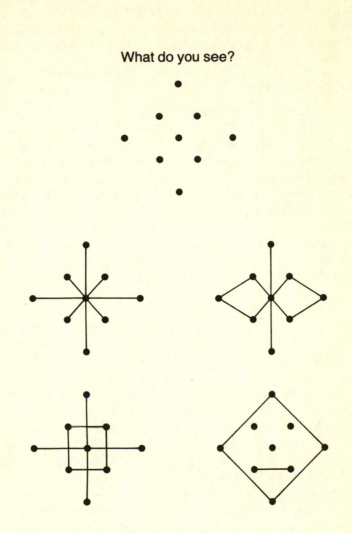

Figure 1.4 Constructive paradigms

for an extensive model which may include many paradigms. In this text we shall use the term 'paradigm' to mean a component idea within a worldview, and so it will be used interchangeably with the terms 'worldview theme' and 'mental model'.

Worldview is learned

We must now turn to the question of how an individual acquires his or her worldview. The fourth characteristic of worldview is that it is learned unconsciously in early life as a person acquires their culture. A child may be said to be born cultureless and yet in a few years quickly begins to develop the skills to interact with his environment in a socially acceptable way. This is most clearly seen in the way that a baby learns to speak and communicate with others. This process of conditioning continues throughout our lives and gradually these learned patterns become the habits which guide our lives. These habits allow us to predict the behaviour of others, and enable us to cope successfully with the environment in which we live.

Not only does a child learn what clothes to wear, or where and how to shake hands, but also the paradigms by which the behaviour makes sense as well. Hand shaking in the socially approved manner achieves good social relationships which are advantageous to the individual. Take the well known story of the three little pigs. In learning the story the child is not merely acquiring a story about one pig who made his house of hay, a second who made his house of wood, and a third who made his of bricks. The child is learning what the particular society regards as being socially valuable. The social principle is that hard work is rewarded by success.

This process is known as 'enculturation'. It has two important repercussions which result from the fact that the majority of people are brought up in just one culture. The first is one which we have already referred to: that is, we tend to be unaware of our own worldview. We are born into cultures just as we are born into the atmosphere of planet earth. The air makes life possible, and yet it is unnoticed by us until we meet another atmosphere. We leave a crowded room, and suddenly become aware of how hot and stuffy the air actually was. We leave the fresh air of the countryside and cough in the smog-clouded air of the city, but in a short time we no longer notice the air. Likewise, culture with its worldview becomes visible on the boundary, and in comparison with others.

We are unaware of how we have acquired our worldview, like the little English boy who was puzzled at the struggles that a Korean gentleman was having with speaking English. 'What's the problem?' he asked, 'All I have to do is open my mouth and English comes out.' The boy did not understand how he was able to speak English because it was so much part of him and his up-bringing. Similarly, it is difficult for an adult to appreciate the assumptions which he or she may hold about the world.

Worldview has therefore been likened to coloured glass through which people see themselves and the world around them.[12] Everything is given the 'tint' of the particular 'glass of the worldview' the person happens to be wearing. As the majority of people are used to just one pair of glasses from their earliest childhood, they are unaware of their actual existence. If they were to change their glasses they would wish to revert to their original glasses for a 'true' perspective of the universe and reality.

A major repercussion of the process of enculturation is that because we are so familiar with particular patterns and ideas we assume that they are the best and most logical. For example, when an Englishman first tries to eat with chopsticks he quickly comes to the conclusion that a knife and fork is much easier to use. This is because he has been brought up to be familiar with the use of the knife and fork and so he has developed the needed dexterity. The same happens to a Chinese gentleman seeking to eat with a knife and fork for the first time. Both men will quickly conclude that their own ways are best. This attitude is known amongst all societies, and is known as 'ethnocentrism', or more simply 'cultural pride'.

This sense of pride not only applies to patterns of behaviour such as methods of eating, but the interpretation and evaluation of experiences. It seems right and logical to interpret these experiences within the context of the worldview with which we are familiar. People who interpret the same experiences in a different way seem 'illogical', just like the anthropologist and the Yap islanders who were making totally different assumptions about the nature of humans compared to pigs. The anthropologist assumed:

1) humans are animals and so are pigs,
2) pigs breed through sexual relations, therefore
3) humans breed through sexual relations.

The Yap islanders did not make assumption one, and so could not go on to make assumptions two and three. Even after they had come to realise the problem of their mutual misunderstanding, both parties regarded their own interpretation as being the most logical and the other strange and foreign. As a writer in *Time* magazine once expressed it: 'We are all captives of the pictures in our heads.'[13]

Patterns for action

If one's worldview is so pervasive, it must be realised that people have a deep commitment to the worldview of the culture in which they have been brought up. People accept the mental model they have and act in accordance with that perspective. Any new information must be interpreted in terms of that model. As Kraft has said, 'The model "tells one," as it were, which of the things that happen to oneself to believe, which not to believe (or even notice), and how to interpret both.'[14] People are therefore reluctant to change their worldview unless it proves totally inadequate to help them cope with their current situation.

The kinds of experiences that human beings face have to be accounted for and explained by their worldview. Stable, repetitive experiences merely reinforce the traditional worldview. When experiences become unpredictable according to the traditional worldview, thinking people in a society will question the traditions of the ancestors.

Thomas Kuhn has argued that such a commitment to accepted paradigms is found in the scientific community.[15] The discovery that the world was not flat but spherical, and that the sun revolved around the earth produced dramatic changes in European thought. Newton's work in mechanics, for instance, was the central paradigm of scientists for two centuries. It provided a practical model to explain the universe, and it was not until a considerable body of information was amassed which did not fit the model that a shift was made to a new model. Einstein's model of relativity has provided a more successful paradigm in explaining recent, but not all scientific discoveries.

Drastic changes in experience lead people to try and create new meanings that will help them cope with the changes. In the past, societies have interacted only with neighbouring cultures, and often this was limited, as in the case of isolated tribal peoples. With the growth of empires, the contact increased and ideas and information began to flow. The Arabic language provided a great highway of information throughout the Muslim world from Mauritania to Indonesia. The formation of the Colonial Empires of the nineteenth century brought European nations into close contact with African and Asian cultures. Today we are experiencing the greatest contact and interaction between societies which has ever occurred. The nation states of the world have all become multi-cultural, causing national tension. The USSR is seeing an unprecedented rise of ethnic feelings which has superseded acceptance of socialist ideas of the unity of the proletariat. The million or more Muslims currently resident in the UK illustrate the multi-cultural nature of Britain.

This growing interaction is not merely a matter of different behaviour, but of different worldviews. The Pakistani Muslim in Britain does not merely have different customs from his white neighbour, but different perceptions of what the world is like. His children find themselves in the midst of a clash which requires them not only to choose different customs, but different sets of values and ideas. Many Pakistani teenagers feel like a person studying the illusion of Figure 1.2. They can make sense of the world in two different ways, but which should they accept? On an individual level, this is the clash of worldviews which all people are facing today.

Notes

1. Whiteman, Darrell. *Melanesians and Missionaries* (William Carey Library: Pasadena, 1983) p 478.
2. Sire, James W. *The Universe Next Door* (IVP: Leicester, 1976) p 17.
3. Luzbetak, Louis J. *The Church and Cultures* (Divine Word Publications: Techny, 1970) p 57.
4. Benedict, Ruth. *Patterns of Culture* (Routledge & Kegan Paul: London, 1961).
5. Opler, Morris E. 'Themes as Dynamic Forces in Culture' *American Journal of Sociology* Vol 51 (1945) pp 198–206.
6. Redfield, Robert. *The Primitive World and Its Transformation* (Cornell University Press: Ithaca, 1953) pp 85–86.
7. Fontaine, Jean La. *What is Social Anthropology?* (Edward Arnold: London, 1985) p 39.
8. Sapir, Edward. *Culture, Language and Personality* (University of California Press: Berkeley, 1958) p 16.
9. Wagner, Peter. *How to Have a Healing Ministry Without Making Your Church Sick* (Monarch: Eastbourne, 1988) p 143.
10. Hiebert, Paul. *Cultural Anthropology* (Lippincott: Philadelphia, 1976) p 6.
11. Barbour, Ian G. *Myths, Models and Paradigms* (Harper & Row: New York, 1974).
12. Hesselgrave, David. *Communicating Christ Cross-culturally* (Zondervan: Grand Rapids, 1978) p 125.
13. *Time* Dec 2, 1985.
14. Kraft, Charles. *Christianity and Culture* (Orbis Books: Maryknoll, 1981) p 28.
15. Kuhn, Thomas. *The Structure of Scientific Revolutions* (University of Chicago Press: Chicago, 1962).

2

EXPLORING OTHER WORLDS

Once upon a time, there was an anthropologist who wanted to study accents in the northern part of his country. He decided that he would visit some of the more remote villages, and ask the people about their accents. He finally arrived at a very isolated village, and soon got into conversation with a local man. This man clearly had a very distinct accent, and the anthropologist began to ask him about it. The man looked puzzled, and denied that he had an accent. The anthropologist went on to another man, and asked him how he pronounced his vowels so that he could make a record of them. This man also looked puzzled at the stranger. Some small boys who had been watching all this activity came over to the anthropologist, and asked, 'Aye Mister, why does you speak in such a funnie waay?'

As we have seen, the problem with worldview is the same as with an accent: you only become aware of it when you come in contact with someone who is different from yourself. This then raises the problem of how one comes to understand a worldview. One cannot just go up to a person and ask them to explain their worldview. A philosopher or theologian may be able to explain some of their beliefs and assumptions, but worldview is more than a system of philosophy or religion. A worldview is something held by everyone in a society. Some people may be able to articulate its nature better than others, but all have a worldview: the schooled and the unschooled, the rich and the poor, the literate and the illiterate.

In this chapter we shall look at four major questions concerning the understanding of worldview. First, how may one seek to gain an understanding of the worldview of another society? Secondly, how do worldviews relate within complex societies? Thirdly, what are the characteristics of a successful worldview? And finally, how may one compare and contrast worldviews?

Understanding another worldview

The first rule in seeking to gain an understanding of another worldview is to engender a climate which enables a person to express their views freely. Any sense of criticism or incredulity can lose the trust and confidence of people. In Africa I often found that the local people were hesitant to speak about ghosts or spirits because Westerners have laughed at their views. Comments such as, 'You cannot still believe in ghosts in this modern world!', make people reluctant to express their real feelings and beliefs. It is necessary to learn to accept another person's perspective of reality as being valid and reasonable. This does not mean that you have to accept their perspective, or even agree with it, but it does mean that you are seeking to appreciate how they perceive the world.

From this starting point, and after much careful study, it is possible to gather valuable clues to worldview themes. The following are a few useful questions which have been derived from original suggestions by Luzbetak.[1]

1)   What beliefs are strongly held?

What are people convinced of as being facts for which they would argue? Do they consider that if you travelled far enough you would fall off the edge of the earth, or do they believe that you would end up back where you started? Do they believe in the existence of a Creator God or not?

2)   How do parents teach children to behave?

Do parents insist on children washing their hands after going to the toilet? This may show that the older generation has the belief in minute creatures, smaller than the eye can detect, causing human sickness. In parts of Africa, parents may scold their children for walking behind them. This is because they are fearful that the child may walk on their shadow and so cause harm to the person.

3) *What do people regard as major offences (sins)?*

In Western society, murder, rape and armed robbery are considered major offences, whilst in other societies hospitality and generosity are important aspects of good behaviour. In some societies, adultery is considered a small sin, whilst neglecting to make an offering to the ancestors is considered to be a major offence.

A story is told by Brian Woodford, of a Birifor Christian preaching to his own people in Ghana.[2] The man was preaching with great fervour on the biblical account of David's adultery with Bathsheba. He then went on to speak about David's great repentance as seen in Psalm 51. He concluded by saying, 'See how great was David's repentance for such a little sin.'

4) *What do people do in crises?*

If there is no rainfall, what do people do? The Karimojong of Uganda will call together the members of the clan, and under the directions of an elder they will perform a rain-making ritual. This will be the offering of an animal as a sacrifice, and praying to a deity believed to live in the sky and called 'Akuj'.[3] In other societies, specialists may charter an aircraft to fly over the clouds and spray dry-ice into the atmosphere in order to precipitate rainfall.

5) *What rituals do people perform?*

Within a Christian society, after a child is born, he or she may be taken to church to be dedicated to God. This immediately shows something of how the people conceive of Deity, and the desire of the parents for the child to be brought up as a member of the Christian community.

6)   *Who are the trend-setters?*

Which people are the models for young people? Who is most admired? Who are the heroes of the society? In Western society, characters such as James Bond, Indiana Jones, Madonna and other personalities of the mass media tend to be opinion leaders. Amongst the Masai of Kenya, the man who is admired is the warrior who has killed a lion.

7)   *What are the greatest fears that people have?*

A Brahman may fear becoming polluted through contact with an untouchable, and for this reason would not drink from the same cup nor eat from the same bowl. In Africa, people may be fearful of walking in the forest at night because evil spirits may attack them. In the Western world, young people may fear growing old, whilst in most of the world, age is respected and admired.

8)   *What are considered to be words of wisdom?*

Often good advice on how to live is presented in the form of proverbs or myths. However, one must take care in their interpretation because proverbs are usually expressed in a symbolic form. For example, a common Haitian proverb says, 'Dirty clothes are washed within the family.' In this case the symbolism is obvious, but in some cases it is more hidden. Take for example the Masai proverb, 'The neck cannot rise above the head.' It means a son should not disobey his father.

9)   *What is expressed in the art forms of the people?*

Art, whether in the form of drama, paintings or music can express much about the values of a people. Islamic art does not allow the representation of any human or animal forms, but encourages the use of calligraphy based upon the Qur'an. This is because of the danger of the sin of 'shirk' which is the making of anything to appear the equivalent of God. On the other hand, Hindu art shows a glorious confusion of humans, animals and gods.

10)   What aspects of the culture are most resistant to change?

Generally, practices relating closely to worldview are most resistant to change. 'In the parched farmlands of northeast Brazil a health worker found it especially difficult to persuade mothers to seek help for their sick children during the month of May. This is because in Catholic teachings May is the "month of the Virgin Mary", and in this part of Brazil it is believed that when a child dies in May it is particularly fortunate, since the Virgin is "calling" her children to come to be with her. To seek medical aid during this time would be to contravene the will of the Virgin.'[4]

These are a few of the many clues which can allow one to draw up a framework of worldview themes. As one becomes increasingly familiar with the particular culture, it is possible to refine the analysis. The themes should be constantly checked and reviewed through new observations, and revised wherever necessary. The observer must always realise that he is a product of his own worldview, and should base his conclusions as much as possible on actual cases rather than his own imagination.

Worldviews in complex societies

Within small communities speaking only one language, there is essentially one common worldview to which all members adhere. In larger societies consisting of millions of people there emerges a plurality of worldviews. It is usually possible to identify certain dominant worldview themes which are accepted by all people living within the particular society.

Within British society one can identify several inter-relating philosophies and religions. One person may claim to be a Marxist, another a materialist, and yet another a Christian. All three are able to cope reasonably well within their common society whilst holding some quite distinct views on certain issues. This is achieved through conformity to the general culture of the society, seen in matters of dress and obedience to a common set of social laws. Their various worldviews may be likened to overlapping circles which contain much common ground.

Where there is a distinct minority culture within a larger social group, the minority faces two options. First, they may be marginalised from the main community. In North America, the European peoples settled the indigenous Indians in reservations where they were isolated from the dominant culture. Secondly, the minority must adopt the majority culture in its wider social relations whilst retaining its own culture in the home. We will return to these various interactions later in this book.

Some writers have a greater hope for mankind, with a vision of people being freed from the restraints of a mono-cultural perspective. Is it possible for individuals to have not just one worldview, but to operate within the framework of two or more? Before we are able to comment upon this vision we first have to look at a few of the major worldviews found in the world.

Characteristic functions of a worldview

As we have seen on many occasions, a worldview is not something which is tangible, which can be weighed and measured, compared and analysed in physical terms. Worldview is a way of perceiving and making sense of the information from the world about us. It is not possible to say that one worldview is true and all others are wrong. Because we are limited cultural beings we cannot comprehend all reality so we must construct mental models (paradigms) in an attempt to cope with the life which we know and experience. We need to ask the question, which model is best? As James Sire has written:

Whatever worldview we adopt will be limited. Our finitude as human beings, whatever our humanity turns out to be, will keep us from both total accuracy in the way we grasp and express our worldview and from completeness and exhaustiveness. Some truths will slip through our finest intellectual nets, and our nets will have some holes we have not even noticed. So the place to start is in humility.[5]

As we have seen already, worldview is the set of preconceived ideas of a people which allows them to cope reasonably success-fully in the world. It is a society's basic model of reality. According to Charles Kraft, worldview serves five major func-tions.[6] By looking at these functions we are able to gain some idea of the qualifications for a satisfactory worldview.

1) The first function of worldview is to explain how and why the world came to be as it is, and how it continues. In other words, a worldview must answer many of the basic questions of life in a way that allows a person, and society to cope with reasonable success. This must happen in four major areas of life.

First, a worldview must meet the biological needs of a soci-ety. Food, water, air, warmth, and protection are essential if a society is to survive. The secular worldview has been outstand-ingly successful at this level, and this has been its main attrac-tion to other societies.

However, a satisfactory life requires more than just the meeting of biological needs, since humans are social beings, and meaningful social relations are essential. The *second* aspect therefore is that of the family and community. A failure at this level can have tragic repercussions: rape, murder, abuse, loneliness, and anarchy.

Thirdly, there is the need for psychological satisfaction. Every individual within a society needs to have his, or her, felt-needs met to an acceptable degree. There is the need to be loved and accepted. Aesthic expression is also an important requirement.

Fourthly, there is a spiritual requirement in which people have an inner need to find answers from outside their own intellect. Every society on earth has had its own religious beliefs, to such a degree that one can say that humans universally have a religious dimension. All the secular education of the Marxist states has failed to eradicate that which Marx called 'the opiate of the people'.

2)   The worldview of a people must also serve the function of evaluation. A society needs ways of judging and validating different actions and institutions. There must be an answer to the question of how a person understands the suffering and evil in the world. Most cultures do this by referring to the unseen, transcultural world for appropriate sanctions. By commencing from their concept of God, or gods, a people group is able to pronounce certain behaviour and practices 'good' or 'evil'.

3)   The worldview of a people must provide psychological reinforcement during times of crises. When a loved one dies, what answer can be given? This is a major difficulty with the secular worldview because there is little comfort in knowing that there is a certain probability of a person being killed in a road accident, and it just happened that your loved one was there at the time. The cry from the heart remains: why did this have to happen to him, or her?

Crises occur at birth, death, marriage, sickness, planting, harvest, war and other times of uncertainty. These are occasions when there is need for a change of routine and behaviour. It is not surprising, therefore, that many societies have special rituals at these transitions. These allow many people to participate in the transition, such as at a wedding service, an initiation rite, or a harvest festival.

4)   The worldview of a people must function as an integrator. If an explanation is inconsistent and self-contradictory one senses a feeling of dissatisfaction. An explanation of one event should fit into the wider arena of what one assumes to be valid and real. As we saw in the first chapter, one of the primary functions of a worldview is to provide a comprehensive, uniform explanation of reality. The greater number of experiences and observations it can meaningfully explain the

more satisfactory the worldview.

Many tribal worldviews fail because they have no explanation for the technological items that are so much a part of Western culture. The tribe suddenly realises that they are not at the centre of the universe, but are only a small, and possibly insignificant part of the whole of humanity. Their traditional worldview fails to provide answers for the many new items and explanations, and thus results in many internal contradictions which lead to the worldview being ultimately abandoned.

5) The worldview of a people must be adaptable. New information and experiences continually come to any society, and a satisfactory worldview must have the potential to provide meaningful answers. A rigid worldview will eventually break under the strain of historical development. A satisfactory worldview must have the potential of flexibility, and even an elegance of simplicity which allows it to relate to many different cultures. It provides the possibility of growth and change.

Comparing worldviews

In the following chapters we are attempting to do four things. First, the aim is to understand some contemporary worldviews which have influenced millions of ordinary people over many centuries. Secondly, in so doing, it is hoped that the reader will gain a better understanding of his or her own worldview. As we have commented already, it is in leaving the atmosphere of our own culture that we will better understand what that atmosphere is actually like. Thirdly, our aim is to try and understand how these various worldviews are interacting with each other in a multitude of ways. Finally, we are seeking to learn some principles for the communication of the Christian gospel to people of other worldviews.

Every culture has its own worldview, and every sub-culture has its own variation on those themes. There are over 6,000 languages in the world, and the people group using each one of these has its own particular worldview. It is therefore impossible to do more than study a few of the major cultural groups whilst recognising the conglomerate nature of some of the comments made (see Figure 2.1). The author would not want to leave the reader with the impression that all Muslims think exactly alike. There is great variety within the Islamic worldview just as there is within the secularised worldview of Europe. However, one can identify some important themes which allow a better understanding of how Muslims think, and to identify the rationale which they are following.

In making a comparison of any two worldviews, one immediately has the problem of how to explain ideas and values of one culture in a language meaningful to another. In Hinduism, the term *maya* means the illusory nature of the natural world. However, it is difficult to express this concept in ways which are accurately meaningful in the English language. We need to resort to the use of the Sanskrit word, and attempt to define its meaning in English.

In the following comparison of worldview themes these have been classed into six major groups:

1)   The Cosmos – What is reality? How does society understand the nature of the universe in which it exists? Is the material world all that exists, or is there a non-material reality?

2)   Self – What is human? How does the society answer the question, 'Who am I?' What model do members of that society have to understand themselves as persons?

3)   Knowing – What is truth? How does one come to know things about reality? Philosophers call this area of thinking epistemology.

4)   Community – What is society? How do people understand their involvement within the communities in which they exist?

5)   Time – What is time? How is this most obscure component of our existence perceived by the society?

6)   Value – What is good? In every area of human activity, values are involved: moral values, aesthetic values, psychological values, political values, economic values, religious values and so on. The word 'value' is here defined as good ends, ideals we ought to pursue.

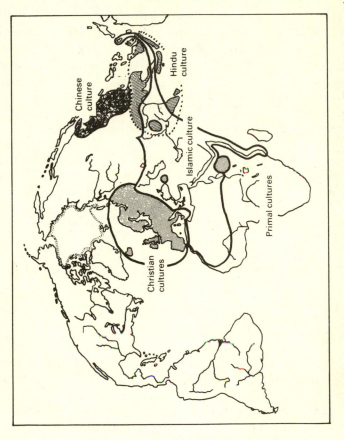

Figure 2.1 The areas of the major cultural traditions prior to the European expansion.

The notions of worldview and paradigm may seem abstruse, but they provide a means by which those living in a multi-cultural world may understand the logic in the thinking of another society. Knowing another culture may free one from or freeze one into the culture of origin. Some people may prefer to cling to their old assumptions whilst others will thrill to the opportunity of exploring strange worlds. I personally believe that it is in appreciating the rationale of another people that Christians are enabled not only to be more effective in their communication, but to understand the nature of their own message more fully. Let us listen to the following words of an old man from the Tewa people of North America.

> It is best to be polite to missionaries, let them come in and preach. We will go on with what we are doing. It is not good to drive anyone away; we must be nice to people no matter who they are. But we feel that no one should disturb what we want to do. If they urge us to listen, we will say nothing. Sometimes they talk a long time telling us that our dances are evil and that we must stop them. They say unless we go the 'Christian Road' we will not be saved. But we just keep quiet and they get tired after a while and leave us alone.[7]

He who knows but one worldview, knows no worldview!

Notes

1. Luzbetak, Lois J. *The Church and Cultures* (Divine Word Publications: Techny, 1970) p 160.
2. Woodford, Brian. WEC missionary working in Ghana.
3. Burnett, David. *Unearthly Powers* (MARC: Eastbourne, 1988) pp 13–14.
4. Foster, George M. *Traditional Societies and Technological Change* (Harper & Row: New York, 1973) p 86.
5. Sire, James. *The Universe Next Door* (IVP: Leicester, 1988).
6. Kraft, Charles. *Christianity and Culture* (Orbis Books: Maryknoll, 1979) pp 54–56.
7. Beals, Alan R. *Culture in Process* (Holt, Reinhart and Winston: New York, 1979) p 318.

PART II
Traditional Worlds

3

MAN AND MACHINES:
The Secular Worldview

One could start with a study of worldviews from any of the major cultures of the world, but most readers of this book are likely to be those from a Western cultural heritage, and so will be most familiar with the secular worldview which has most influenced our own contemporary social history. It is only as we come to understand the assumptions which make up our own worldview that we will be better able to understand others. Referring back to the analogy of the coloured glasses mentioned in the previous chapter, we need to appreciate the tint of our own glasses before we can begin to understand the colour of the glasses other people wear. Yet we will soon start to see that it is only as we begin to understand others that we will more fully appreciate our own assumptions. Thus, we enter into a dynamic interaction. The more we understand our own worldview, the more we can understand another worldview, which in turn will allow a fuller appreciation and understanding of our own worldview.

Although we will commence with the secular worldview, we will continue to refer back to it as we examine other worldviews and develop some of the major themes.

The emergence of the modern form of 'secularism', or 'naturalism' as it has been called by some, occurred in the seventeenth century with thinkers such as René Descartes (1596–1650). He conceived the universe to be an enormous machine which human beings could study. In doing this, Descartes drew a distinction between the 'observer' and the 'object', and thus between 'mind' and 'matter'. This distinction, known as the 'Cartesian dualism', meant that, on one hand the scientists were freed to study the body as part of the total material universe, and on the other, the mind, or soul, was left to the philosophers and theologians. This dualism was an assumption which would have far reaching repercussions as we shall see later.

John Locke (1632–1704) was a second writer of note. Like Descartes, he would confess to a belief in God, but took Descartes' views a stage further with the assumption that man's reason was to be taken as judge of what was actually true. 'I am because I think' became the basis of logic. Knowledge, it was assumed, comes through the medium of the physical senses. Revelation was therefore demoted and even discarded, and reason made the sole criterion for the truth concerning reality. The outcome was that reality was considered to be composed of only matter, and that included man himself. Descartes and Locke thus laid the foundation for a new worldview with an emphasis upon matter, and with the metaphor of the machine.

Who has not been fascinated by the ingenuity of a clockwork machine? The gears and cogs moving with precision and order both impress and provide the stimulus for newer machines. The machine model for a worldview therefore likens the universe to a gigantic clock. Its acceptance within European society only further stimulated the technological revolution of the nineteenth century.

This worldview has proved to be most successful in many areas, and has developed in various forms. Secular humanism was important in the nineteenth century, along with Deism, its theological counterpart. Hedonism has proved to be another important manifestation especially within Western society, whilst Marxism has dominated the Communist countries. Many common themes can be identified in these various expressions.

Secular worldview themes

The Cosmos

Matter exists and is all that does exist. This assumption is the basis of what in philosophy is called 'Materialism' – the physical and natural world is real and orderly and can be experienced through the senses. This worldview strongly affirms the reality of the material world, but as we shall see this contrasts markedly with the Hindu worldview, for example. This world-affirming assumption has some important corollaries.

First, there is a categorical distinction between the natural world and the imaginations created by the human mind. There is a distinction between fact and fiction, awake experiences and dreams, history and myth. The natural world is directly experienced through the senses and can therefore be measured and studied. This focus upon the natural order is one of the strengths of the secular worldview, and has resulted in man's increasing control over his environment.

Secondly, the universe is not open to interference or control from outside. It is a total, self-sufficient unit – a 'closed' system. There are no gods, ghosts, or spirits existing in an unseen world which can affect the lives of human beings. I remember an African telling the story of a man who was approached by a snake which spoke to him, making an offer that if he would worship the snake, the snake would make him rich. A European overhearing the story laughed at the thought of a snake talking. To him it was incredible that such a thing could occur. The African did not laugh!

Thirdly, the universe is seen as consistent and orderly. Changes only take place according to predictable processes and only then within limits. To be believed and accepted as true, any reaction must be reproducible in similar conditions. Everything must follow the laws of cause-and-effect. This is the basis of Newton's 'Laws of Mechanics' which consider the gross motion and inertia of a body. These laws were regarded as being applicable to largest of bodies such as the planets and stars, and also the very smallest. They were also regarded as applying uniformly throughout the whole of the universe, being equally applicable to living beings.

It therefore would be impossible – by contrast with the primal worldview, which will be discussed in the next chapter – for a person to change suddenly into an animal, or fly at night to mysterious gatherings. This emphasis upon the material world that is the main feature of the secular worldview also rules out the possibility of divine intervention. Miracles therefore cannot occur, and any such claims must be studied to find a logical scientific answer for the phenomenon.

A fourth corollary is that there's no God. The first Russian spaceman looked out upon the world and said, 'I cannot see God!' The assumption is that since God cannot be seen and analysed he is not a reality. God, together with concepts of angels, spirits and ghosts, becomes classified as illusion. God is relegated to the same category as Superman, Father Christmas, and fairies. A clear distinction is therefore made between the 'real world', which can be studied scientifically, and imagination and belief that is beyond such analysis.

Therefore, there is one major question to be answered. If God does not exist, how then was the present order formed? If matter is eternal does it mean that the world will always remain as it is? The answer is clearly in the negative. But the theory of evolution as proposed by Charles Darwin, in his book *The Origin of Species* (1859), provided at least a partial answer. Darwin essentially assumed that there is a universal process of development from the simple to the complex. Those organisms which survive are those best adapted to their environment and its requirements for living.

Fifthly, the world is divided into numerous distinct categories. This is exactly what Darwin did in categorising living creatures into distinct species. In the secular worldview, human beings are different from animals, which are different from plants, which in turn are different from insects and material objects like rocks and cars. This leads to numerous differences in how Western society deals with items of the various categories. People, for example, cannot be killed for food whereas animals may. Human knowledge is divided into an endless series of categories: chemistry, physics, mathematics, law, etc.

The Self

The secular worldview sees humanity in the same terms as the cosmos, as in fact do most worldviews. René Descartes popularised the notion that human beings are complex machines, albeit ones inhabited by an immortal soul. One of his near contemporaries, a man named Julien La Mettrie, carried the analogy to its radical conclusion, arguing in his book *L'Homme Machine* (Man the Machine) that even the concept of the soul was superfluous because machines did not have souls. The body is seen as consisting of a complex system of chemicals which react in ways that are not yet fully understood. The mind is seen as a function of the mechanism of the body. Even human feelings and thoughts are the result of the secretion of glands and chemical reactions.

The computer metaphor has not gone unrecognised. Psychologist Richard Gregory has made the distinction between 'hardware' and 'software' as it relates to human beings. The body is the hardware, whilst the thinking processes of the mind are the software. One could argue that the physical brain is the hardware, and that culture (mind) is the software.[1] Human beings are therefore considered as being moulded by their environment almost as a computer which is programmed to react in particular ways to certain stimuli. Anthropologists such as Skinner and White have regarded man as being totally programmed by his culture. 'The individual is merely an organization of cultural forces and elements that have impinged upon him forces from outside and which find their overt expression through him.'[2] Karl Marx also used this concept of man in his theories of class formation.

The mechanical model of man proposed by the secular worldview leads to an individualistic concept of man. Just as a clock can work totally independent of another clock so one person is independent from another person. Once a baby is born any linkage between mother and child is merely social. There is no mystical link with the family lineage as is common in tribal societies. There is no need for honour to be given to the older generation just because they procreated the younger generation. All human beings are equal.

If the human body is considered to be a biological mechanism, it is consistent to consider diseases as physical changes of the biological organism. This may result from an intrusion of germs, the breakdown of the body-machine due to cold, fatigue, or the lack of proper food. To Africans, the Westerner often seems to be unduly concerned with germs and eating proper foods. These may even appear to be irrational ideas in another culture where the clear distinction between man and nature, made by the Westerner, breaks down. Sickness may be considered as being caused by evil spirits. In Ethiopia, an American was perplexed by the fact that a sick child grinding his jaws was looked upon as a sign of the evil eye.[3] Among the nomadic Arabs, it has been very difficult to clean up water holes contaminated with typhoid. Clean water is not desired because the people prefer the strong taste given to the contaminated water by the camels. The drinker is supposed to acquire manly qualities from the water, and no connection is made between water and disease. The latter is the will of God.[4]

Therefore, death, according to the secular worldview, is seen merely as the cessation of chemical processes which produce the awareness of life. There was nothing before the awareness of life, and there is nothing which follows death. Death is merely the end.

Knowing

Fancis Bacon wrote, 'Knowledge is power.' The human mind, with its rational processes, is assumed by the secularist to allow the examination of the universe, and the laws of cause-and-effect by which it is regulated. By manipulating various factors the observer is able to discern effects which allow him to identify real laws by which the universe is controlled. Empiricism, as this assumption is called, is the basis for the growth of modern science.

Empiricism does make two assumptions. First, whatever cannot be shown to register as sensory information, such as mind or spirit, does not exist. Secondly, the observer has no intrinsic influence upon that which is being observed. As we shall see later, this second assumption has some important repercussions with regards to the current growth of the New Age movement.

The knowledge which has arisen from this approach has allowed humans to establish a remarkable degree of control over the natural order. Never before have there been whole societies with adequate food, provision for their physical needs, and leisure. It is not surprising therefore that there is a general belief that all the problems of the world can be solved by technological methods. Thus, President Kennedy made the commitment to the American people in 1960, that by the end of the decade America would have a man on the moon, and reduce world poverty. The first was accomplished, but not the second.

Community

As we have already seen, the great emphasis that the secular worldview places upon the mind of the one who perceives the world leads to a stress upon the individual. A society, or even a family therefore becomes an association of individuals who live together for their mutual cooperation and benefit.

The individuality and worth of each person is accepted as being more important than that of family and social responsibilities. All people are therefore believed to have inalienable rights to their development to their full potential – 'self-actualisation' as Abraham Maslow would speak of it.[5]

Because of the stress upon the individual, a person may develop links with others outside his family which are of equal, or greater importance than those with his own family. Thus, associations and clubs become of great importance to the individual rather than his kinship group. He will spend far more time with friends who have similar interests to his own than with aunts and uncles who are only visited on birthdays and Christmas.

In an African town it is quite common to find a child of a sister or cousin being brought up in a home alongside the children of the close family. In some societies the kinship term that is used for an aunt is the same word as used for the natural mother. Many Africans find it shocking that Western families place their elderly fathers or mothers in old people's homes. As one puzzled old African man once asked me, 'Why do you spend so much time building sky-scrapers when your families are falling apart?'

Time

Like other dimensions of the universe, time is considered to be linear. Time is conceived as stretching from the infinite past into the limitless future. This apparently endless measure of time provides the opportunity for the astronomically large probability figures required for the process of organic evolution.

Time extends without repeating itself. A person has therefore only one life to live, and each second is unique. Time becomes a commodity of great value as it rushes on into the future. 'Time flies!' we say, and 'one has to keep up with the times.' The English language has many expressions revealing the value of time. Time can be 'wasted', 'lost', and above all measured. Clocks abound within Western societies. Many tribes-people shake their heads in wonder at the white man who rushes around in the heat of the day to fulfil his latest project. They wonder why he has no time to greet people properly, and to sit and converse with them. In their society, a man works when he needs to acquire something, like buying a new shirt or growing food. Why does the white man work just because the time is between 9 am and 5 pm?

The secular view of time does, however, have a progressive view of the future which is believed to allow actions to be undertaken at the present time that will affect the future. Thus, most Western people have an optimistic view of the future. It is axiomatic that something which is 'new' is 'better'. Western advertisements play on the theme of 'new', 'better', and 'improved'. In contrast, many peasant societies stress the importance of traditional values. In Thailand there is the proverb, 'If we follow the old people, we will not be bitten by the dog.'

Value

Absolute ethical considerations do not play a role in secularism, because any standards must be formulated within the closed system of the universe. Value judgement must therefore relate to human beings themselves, and to what society considers to be useful and expedient. Ethics are therefore relative. As Redfield has written: 'Cultural relativism means that the values expressed in any culture are to be both understood and themselves valued only according to the way the people who carry that culture see things.'[6]

Laws and ethical values are based upon man-made assumptions. They are necessary only in so far that they allow the individuals within a society to develop their own potential without detriment to others. The judgement of what is right and wrong can only be made with regards to a particular context. It is often known as 'situational ethics'.

Individuals living within the material world seek to achieve their full potential by the control of elements within the universe. This leads to a competitive attitude towards other people, and an aggressive policy towards the material world. Human beings are said to 'conquer space', and 'subdue nature'. American advisors working in Laos could not get over the lack of competitive spirit amongst village people. When Americans play volleyball, they aim to win even though it is only a game. Amongst the Lao, they would have teams, but they played to enjoy the game, and did not care who won.[7]

The secular worldview is one which is optimistic and confident in human initiative. Progress in human control over nature is regarded as being assured. There are two major forms of this worldview common in the world. The first is secular humanism which has been basically outlined previously. This considers humanity to be essentially good, and the acquisition of material goods as being a worthwhile end in itself. The other major form of this worldview is expressed in the philosophies owing their origin to Karl Marx.

Marxism

One of the most significant forms of the secular worldview has been that of Karl Marx (1818–83), whose ideas have been an inspiration for many. Not only was Marx a materialist, but he also applied the theory of dialectics. Dialectics owed its development to the German philosopher Friedrich Hegel (1770–1830). Hegel said that everything in the natural world and society is in a constant process of change. Nothing remains exactly the same from one moment to the next. This continual motion is the product of a constant conflict between opposing forces, the 'thesis' and the 'antithesis', which produced a 'synthesis', which in turn would bring forth its negation, and conflict.

Hegel thought that the world was developing according to a preordained master plan of God ('absolute spirit') which man was trying to carry out. Marx acclaimed Hegel's theory of the dialectical process, but he disagreed with Hegel that men's ideas were inspired by a master plan. Men's ideas, Marx argued, were shaped by the cultural environment into which he was born.

For Marx, history was a continuing process, just as every living thing in nature was part of a continuing process of evolution. The motive force in that process, in history as in nature, was the interaction of opposing forces. The opposing forces in history were opposing social classes.

In ancient times, men roamed freely over the earth as hunter/gatherers. As populations grew, humans were forced to develop tools to exploit the natural resources around them more effectively. Gradually, a division of labour arose to provide ways of more effectively exploiting these resources. Each man specialised in different forms of work which he did most of the time. Eventually, this division of labour extended to society as a whole: one class ruled, whilst the other obeyed orders. From the time of earliest civilisations, society was divided into such classes. Each ruling class controlled the mode of production – that is, the way of exploiting the natural resources.

As human knowledge of science developed, each mode of production in turn became out-dated. Those who benefited from the old system inevitably tried to hold back the progress of more sophisticated means of production. Change had to take place. One of the oppressed groups would take power from the ruling class in a revolution, and establish a new more efficient mode of production. For Marx, the economic system of capitalism was not an eternal system, but only the latest in a succession of different systems.

Capitalism had its origin, according to Marx, in the trade and commerce organised by the merchant class under the feudal regimes of medieval Europe. With the European expansion of the sixteenth and seventeenth centuries, they returned with great wealth which enriched the merchant classes at home. The accumulation of riches enabled the merchants to finance manufacturing enterprises, which gradually expanded into large scale industries. The merchants therefore became a class of industrialists who rebelled against the old means of production, represented by the feudal aristocracy, whose power was based upon land ownership.

Marx believed that social changes occurred when a new mode of production developed which was more efficient than the previous. Slavery gave way to feudalism, and this in turn had to give way to capitalism with its industry and factories. Up to a certain point, Marx argued, capitalism was a progressive force, because it organised the use of resources more effectively than the old feudal system. However, he believed that capitalism was doomed because of a basic contradiction: the capitalist must continue to produce more and more goods, or else go out of business. Sooner or later, a point is reached where the market for the products is too small to provide a sufficient profit.

Marx explained that industrialists make their profits from the exploitation of the working class. The growth of industry under capitalism was bringing more and more workers together, often thousands in one large factory. Eventually, these workers would unite into a powerful force which would overthrow the capitalists.

> The immediate aim of the Communists is...the formation of the proletariat into a class, the overthrow of bourgeois supremacy, and the conquest of the political power by the proletariat. The Communists disdain to conceal their views and aims. They openly declare that their ends can be attained only by the forcible overthrow of all existing social conditions. Let the ruling classes tremble at a Communistic revolution. The proletarians have nothing to lose but their chains. They have a world to win.[8]

For Marx, the proletarian revolution would be different from any previous revolution. In the past, one class overthrew a rival oppressing class and became in its turn the oppressor. The proletarian revolution would be the great majority of the people, not the minority. This would abolish the whole basis of the class system, and a new classless society would emerge. From this classless society would emerge a new type of man, free from the cultural influences of a class ridden society. This 'new man' would not be so individualistic or competitive, but would work on the basis, 'From each according to his abilities, to each according to his needs.'[9]

The expansion of the secular worldview

The secular worldview grew rapidly in the nineteenth century, and dominated the universities and centres of Western philosophy. It provided the basic assumptions for most scientific study with resulting technological developments that led to the expansion of the European peoples. It is true to say that the secular worldview has been the most powerful and influential of any worldview in recent centuries. Its influence has reached some of the most isolated societies, and has resulted in great changes within the worldviews of other major societies.

Why has the secular worldview had such an influence in the twentieth century? First, the technological developments resulting from the secular worldview have, without doubt, been spectacular. Technology has given to Western society military and political domination over much of the globe. This showed itself particularly with the establishment of the colonial empires. It has given a level of comfort for the individual which has never been known before. Western man is perceived by other societies to have an abundance of food, shelter, and convenience. Whilst tribal man struggles to grow sufficient food with back-breaking effort, Western man knows no shortage and seems to apply little effort to obtain what he wants. He rides in air-conditioned cars whilst the peasant walks in the hot sun. He has clean comfortable houses whilst the peasant struggles to build a simple shelter for his family.

Secondly, this evident success of Western man has produced a sense of confidence and superiority. Vast numbers of people have therefore accepted this worldview as being a complete, satisfactory, and coherent model for human living. It seems to give to man a position of dignity and self-esteem. Man is able to control nature to meet his individual needs and desires.

The secular worldview, therefore, expanded from out of Europe to influence most other societies of the world. This caused various reactions to these new ideas. The first was that some people in almost every society were converted to secular philosophy. Thus, today one can find a 'secularised', or 'Westernised' segment within most societies. It is often this group which has gained political power in the newly formed nation state. They seek for the same level of wealth and prosperity seen in the Western nations. They desire the technological items which would make life more comfortable for their own people.

These people have sought to deal with their new experiences by converting from their traditional worldview to the apparently more successful secular worldview. Western people have encouraged this process by making available knowledge, the new power, through schools and universities. This has especially been influential upon the young, who have eagerly devoured the new knowledge. Their parents who encouraged them in these studies did not realise that with the knowledge came new ways of conceiving the world. Children were educated out of their traditional worldview into the Western worldview. Traditional society was fractured as the younger generation split from the older. Youth, with its new knowledge, began to despise the old.

To me this was epitomised in one young boy at a residential primary school in northern Kenya. He was a Turkana, a pastoral people, who wandered the rift valley with their camels, sheep and goats. When I asked him where his father was he scowled, and said, 'He is with his animals, but he is nothing.' The son despised his father and had the ambition to be a teacher and wear Western clothes.

The frustration of many in the Third World when seeing the rapidly increasing wealth of Western nations has led to an acceptance of Marxist principles. 'Revolution' has been taken as the key to material prosperity. Many nations have been disappointed to find that revolution has not been able to provide the answers, and in the process, much of their cultural heritage has been destroyed.

Weaknesses of the secular worldview

Despite its obvious success in technological development secularism has had many critics. Christians have always been foremost amongst these, but during the twentieth century an increasing number of others have pointed out that scientific objectivity fails to answer several important questions in the following areas.

Meaning

The secular worldview fails to recognise that as a person I must have meaning and purpose for life. 'Why am I here?' is a question to which all people require an answer. Yet, to this question the secular worldview gives no answer.

Various philosophers have sought to find an answer. Nihilism has been proposed as one answer. Friedrich Nietzsche refers to the surging energies within man which overcome the static and the weak. In his book *Thus Spake Zarathrustra*, Nietzsche pictures an old man travelling the towns and villages of Eastern Europe, telling the news that God is dead. 'Whatever shall we do?' people ask. To which the old man replies, 'Let your will now say, man shall be the meaning of the earth!'[10]

Community

The relativistic ethics of the secular worldview provide no practical advice for governments trying to provide law and order for its citizens, especially in a multi-cultural state. Who says what is right? There must be rules to allow communal living, but from where does the authority for these rules derive? Many governments have therefore moved to a totalitarian position, where a small élite make decisions which are binding on all within society irrespective of culture. This eventually leads to a democratic movement seeking for more personal freedom. Once the authoritative rule is relaxed, the inter-cultural tensions emerge often with violent results.

Transcendental Experience

The secular worldview stresses logical analysis, but human beings also experience emotions and intuition. How can one make sense of these? Existentialism represents one such attempt. It accepts that nothing is of value in the objective world, and that the individual must strive to create value. As James Sire describes the approach, 'The person who lives an authentic existence is the one who keeps ever aware of the absurdity of the cosmos but who rebels against that absurdity and creates meaning.'[11] How can such a leap into the dark provide any answer?

Ecological Crises

The growth of industrialisation which has grown along with the secular worldview has resulted in major ecological problems. Human mastery of the world has led to explosive population growth, decreasing resources and increasing pollution. The growing 'green consciousness' illustrates how many are seeing the weaknesses of a runaway secular worldview.

Einstein and the Theory of Relativity

The basic postulate of Einstein's theory of relativity is that the laws of science should be the same for all freely moving observers, no matter what their speed. This was true for Newton's laws of motion, but was extended to include the speed of light. All observers should measure the same speed of light, no matter how fast they are moving. This simple idea had some remarkable consequences; the best known are that nothing may travel faster than the speed of light, and the equation $E=mc^2$ (where E is energy, m is mass and c is the speed of light).

The consequences of this assumption have had a revolutionary effect on the ideas of space and time. The theory of relativity puts an end to the idea of absolute time. Consider a pair of twins. If one twin went on a long trip in a spaceship at nearly the speed of light, then when he returned to earth he would be much younger than the one who stayed behind. This is known as the twins paradox, but it is a paradox only if one assumes the idea of absolute time.

Einstein did not finish here. He rejected Newton's ideas of gravity as a force between two bodies, and recast it in terms of a 'field' arising from a four-dimensional space-time continuum, itself induced by the presence of matter.[12] On earth, the practical repercussions are usually negligible, but astronomical phenomena may be more accurately predicted and explained by Einstein than by Newton. A small deviation in the orbit of Mercury that could not be accounted for in terms of Newtonian mechanics could be explained in relativistic terms. Similarly the bending of starlight by the sun was predicted, and during a total eclipse of 1918, was triumphantly recorded by Eddington.[13]

Newtonian mechanics assumes that one can apply the basic law of mechanics to any and every situation within the universe. However, atomic physics has shown that these laws cannot and do not apply at the atomic level because it is impossible to know both the momentum and position of an atomic particle with sufficient accuracy. This is generally known as the Heisenberg uncertainty principle.[14] To try and describe these particles, a new approach has developed known as 'Quantum Mechanics'. For our present study, what is more important than the new mathematical approach which Quantum Mechanics offers is the realisation by scientists of the limitations of human observational powers.

What has happened is that new discoveries have shown the weakness of the Newtonian model of the universe, and with it the secular worldview. This has resulted in a paradigm shift within Western society from a Newtonian to an Einsteinian model. We will return to the contemporary relevance of this point in the chapter which examines the New Age movement.

The contrast between differing worldviews is sharply evident as we turn our attention to a very different worldview – that of primal societies.

Notes

1. Schultz, Emily A. and Lavenda, Robert H. *Cultural Anthropology: A Perspective on the Human Condition* (West Publishing Company: S Paul, 1987) p 162.

2. White, Leslie. *The Science of Culture* (Farrar, Strauss and Company: New York, 1949).

3. Stewart, Edward C. *American Cultural Patterns: A Cross-Cultural Perspective* (Intercultural Network Inc.: Illinois, 1972) p 88.

4. Hall, Edward T. *The Silent Language* (Anchor Press: New York, 1973) pp 101–2.

5. Cosgrove, Mark P. *Psychology Gone Awry* (IVP: Leicester, 1982), pp 70–72.

6. Nida, Eugene A. *Customs and Cultures* (Harper & Brothers: New York, 1954), p 49.

7. Stewart, *op cit*, p 43.

8. Marx, Karl. *The Communist Manifesto*.

9. Marx, *ibid*.

10. Nietzsche, Friedrich. *Thus Spake Zarathustra* (Macmillan: New York, 1902) pp 1–10.

11. Sire, James W. *The Universe Next Door* (IVP: Leicester, 1988)
p 115.

12. Peacock, Roy E. *A Brief History of Eternity* (Monarch: Eastbourne, 1989) pp 54–55.

13. Hawking, Stephen W. *A Brief History of Time* (Bantam Press: London, 1988) p 31.

14. Hawking, *ibid* p 55.

4

PRINCIPALITIES AND POWERS
The Primal Worldview

> I was born in Jaltal, an ailing child with a great head that caused my mother much pain. While I was still in the womb, my father mistook a snake for a bit of wood and struck it with his axe. This snake was really the God Ajorasum, and when I was born he made me very ill. But my father called a shaman, who sacrificed a fowl to the angry god and dedicated a pot with many promises and I recovered. Later, when I was old enough to play with other children and take the cattle out to graze, my father sacrificed a buffalo to Ajorasum on the bank of a stream.[1]

This story comes from one of the many villages in India, and illustrates a radically different worldview from that of the secular West. Various terms have been used to designate this way of understanding the world: 'tribal', 'polytheistic', 'primitive' and 'animistic', amongst others. It is difficult to find a term which will please everyone. We will be using the term 'primal' which has been proposed by Harold Turner for those religions which 'both anteceded the great historic religions and continue to reveal many of the basic and primary features of religion.'[2] As we shall soon see, this definition allows one to apply the concepts not only to isolated tribal societies, but also to pagan beliefs which are currently emerging within Western society.

Before the growth of the major world religions, the primal religions appeared to influence all human societies. Each people group seemed to have its own particular religious expression. It is therefore necessary to speak of primal religions, the addition of the plural 's' being deliberate, as they cannot be regarded as just one religion. For example, the Ewe of

Ghana had their particular religion, the Masai of East Africa had their own religion, and the Naga of India theirs. Linked with each religion, one could identify a particular worldview, but in practice one would find many common themes. These themes may be compared and contrasted with those of the other major worldviews found in the world. This process is vulnerable to the criticism of oversimplification, but it does provide the framework for the overarching comparison of major worldviews which we are currently trying to make. We will therefore speak of 'the primal worldview', but as with the other major worldviews that are being considered, one would ask the reader to bear in mind that this term encompasses a set of similar but distinct worldviews belonging to particular people groups.

The growth of the major world religions such as Hinduism, Christianity and Islam saw many societies converted from their primal views. The result is that today the primal worldview prevails mainly in sub-Saharan Africa, the Pacific Islands, the Amazonian Indians, and isolated peoples of Asia. This conversion process was never total with the result that many people who would call themselves followers of major world religions are in practice adherents of a 'primal worldview'. It is for this reason that Stephen Neil estimates that the worldview of at least 40% of the world's population is basically of this form.[3]

Characteristics of the primal worldview

The Cosmos

The primary characteristic of this worldview is that the whole of the created universe is considered to be a total unity. The non-material components of the universe are equally as real and valid as are the material components. To employ the term used in the discussion of the secular worldview, the primal worldview is not a closed system. No dichotomy exists between the sacred and the profane. It is this sacralism which unifies experience and homogenises primal societies.

The universe is considered to have been created by, and is continually influenced by, spiritual beings who are part of this unseen world. A Supreme Creator is a common concept amongst most tribal societies, but this Creator is regarded as being distant from human beings and having little concern for them. There are an abundance of myths and stories which tell of how the Creator God withdrew from his creation. The Tiv of Nigeria know God as Aondo.

> In the beginning Aondo dwelt near the earth and personally watched over it. One day, however, as a woman was preparing food by pounding yams in her mortar, she struck her pestle against Aondo, and he in hurt anger left the earth and now dwells in the heavens. Indeed, the word for sky is Aondo, and the clouds are his spots.[4]

For the Tiv, Aondo is the inscrutable phenomenon of the universe who abides in distant majesty. This leads to a sense of fatalism so that the Tiv may simply shrug their shoulders in the face of catastrophe, and say, 'It is Aondo.'

This alienation from the supreme Creator means that it is the lesser spiritual beings who most directly influence people. Often these spirits are perceived as having personalities very much like that of humans, being a mixture of both good and evil. Nature spirits are to be found everywhere – in trees, rivers, hills or other natural phenomena. Nature is considered to have a life of its own, and one frequently finds the concept of the Mother Earth goddess who is fertilised by the sky-god.

Nature is influenced by these various spiritual beings and forces which are capricious and able to disturb the balance of nature. Humans must therefore ally themselves with the forces of good which cause the annual cycle of nature to bring forth its harvest. Failure to do so would disturb the balance of nature and bring disaster upon the whole tribe.

Human beings exist in a complex and dangerous world of seen and unseen powers and beings. This contrasts sharply with the secular worldview in which mankind is active, presenting its will upon the material world. Many primal societies seek to live in harmony with nature of which they are merely a part. The Australian Aborigines feel a strong link with the mountains and streams, and the animals and birds. They see themselves as being at one with nature.[5] Other primal societies often see themselves as being in a war, holding back the forces of nature. The Anufo of Ghana burn the bush around their homesteads every year in the dry season to push back the encroaching forest.[6] No wonder such people are amazed at the self-confidence of the Westerner.

The Self

In contrast to the secular worldview, the emphasis in the primal worldview is placed not upon the individual, but upon society as a whole. Thus, it is human society which is placed at the centre of the primal worldview, and not the individual as in the secular worldview.

The inter-penetration of the material and non-material world occurs also within the nature of the individual. The soul of a person is not perceived as being locked within the bodily frame, but having a possible external existence. This concept, usually called by anthropologists the 'external soul', allows for the soul to leave the confines of the body.[7] Sickness, for example, may be diagnosed as being due to the 'loss of the soul'. A sorcerer have may caught the person's soul, with the result that the individual becomes lethargic, sickly, and may even die. The concept of the external soul means that the people can readily accept the ideas of a witch leaving her body at night and flying to do her evil deeds. It explains those strange dreams which seem so real.

The immaterial part of man is not necessarily seen as a total entity. The human soul is understood as several inter-related souls, and not just one, as within Western thinking. This explains why a sorcerer can 'steal' a soul whilst the person still has the ability to live, though with a reduced function.

This theme, therefore, provides an explanation of sickness and healing found in primal societies. If a person's soul is lost, then to be healed, the soul needs to be found and returned.

Sickness may also occur from the intrusion of a spirit into a person, and in this case the spirit must be exorcised. One missionary doctor trying to explain that sickness was a result of germs within the body, had the tribal man look down his microscope. The man responded, 'So, that is what evil spirits look like.'

Within primal societies, healing is often performed by the shaman, such as the one mentioned in the story at the beginning of this chapter.[8] Shamans are usually people who themselves have passed through a period of chronic illness and have often come to the point of death. On recovering they find that they have powers to travel into the spiritual world, and find the lost soul of the sick person, or eat the spirit causing the sickness. As we shall see later, the experiences of the shaman are being incorporated into some streams of the New Age movement in Western societies today.

The concept of the multiple nature of the soul also explains why there is such a strong attachment of an individual to his particular lineage. Some aspect of the ancestor's soul is transmitted to make him the person who he is, and as such he has a responsibility to his ancestors. He is, only because they were. The ancestors are therefore superior to him, and every person has a responsibility to his or her ancestors.

Death is not the end. It is the change of existence in which the person moves from the world of the living to become a part of the world of the ancestors. Elaborate funeral rites are often performed to ensure this incorporation. John Mbiti has called the deceased the 'living dead' in an attempt to illustrate that the unbroken tie with the living remains.[9]

Knowing

Because man lives in a capricious world of hostile spirits, he must follow the well-worn paths of his ancestors. They have learned to live in the world, and have passed on their wisdom in terms of their mythology and rituals. A myth should not be regarded as just a 'fairy-story'. Mythology is for primal societies a way of conveying practical truth and wisdom, but expressed in symbolic terms. To use a familiar English example, we could speak of a proverb such as 'A stitch in time saves nine.' The proverb tells of the wisdom of dealing with a problem before it gets too large and so out of hand. The wisdom is expressed in the symbolic terms of sewing, which makes for easy remembrance. Similarly, myths are truths passed on from generation to generation in terms of verbal symbols. Karl Jung has made a study of many of these symbols in his exploration of archetypes, which will be discussed later.

An important aspect of knowing how to live within the hostile world is to know how to avoid disturbing the spirits, and how to manipulate spiritual powers. The cultic prohibitions (taboos) passed on by the ancestors provide rules which regulate human behaviour so as to avoid upsetting the spirits. If the equilibrium within the world is disturbed, it may be restored by rituals which often involve blood sacrifices. In these ways, the non-material reality can be manipulated and influenced by means of religion and magic. Sir James Frazer defined 'magic' as the use of particular rituals to control various forces to answer the problems of everyday life. He saw magic as being a sort of supplement to the use of technical knowledge to cope with existence. 'Religion', on the other hand, he saw more in terms as a passive appeal to a god or spirit for assistance.[10]

In the primal worldview, there is no event without a spiritual cause, and so the primal man must look beyond physical events. Why is this person sick? Have they been possessed by an evil spirit? Why have the crops not grown even though the farmer has done the same as in previous years? Perhaps it is due to the evil work of a witch? Herein lies the importance of divination within primal societies in providing answers to these questions. To the secular man it may seem that divination is nothing but a psychological technique designed to relieve anxiety, and that is certainly one of the functions of divination. However, this takes divination outside the context of the primal culture and so fails to show its relevance in understanding a mysterious and dangerous world.

If sacrifices are offered to appease the spirits, dreams come from the gods and ancestors to give direction and guidance to the living. Although not every dream is regarded as being of significance within a primal society, many are regarded as being of importance and worthy of discussion with others as to their meaning. Dreams and visions can provide wisdom from the spiritual realm worthy of consideration and action.

Community

Westerners have often been amazed at the depth of commitment that an African would have to his family. This results from the fact that every person is perceived as a participant within a particular society. The value of an individual as a person lies not within himself, but in the fact that he is part of an endless chain of humanity. The life an individual experiences has been passed on from generation to generation through his ancestors, and will continue on in the person's children and grand-children. The person finds individual value in the assumptions, 'I am, because I participate', 'I am, because we are'. This contrasts markedly with the secular worldview which assumes, 'I can reason, therefore I am.' This assumption leads to the individualistic focus within secular cultures.

The stress upon the community means that family obligations take a higher priority than do those of individual desires. The group well-being takes priority over personal happiness. A girl, for example, will be willing to marry a man of her father's choosing because it is for the good of the family. The fact of whether there are feelings of love between the couple plays little part in the arrangement of the marriage.

Because the community is important for the individual's worth, he wants to extend his social links with other groups. He wants to be needed, and participate in the lives of other people. In a primal society it is therefore important to socialise. When a visitor comes to your home, one inquires as to his family, and then only after some time comes to the reason for the visit. The Westerner, on the other hand, comes straight to the point and asks, 'What do you want?' The Western worldview immediately reveals itself in the assumption that the person wants some item owned by the individual. This often causes deep offence to the African or Asian.

Important decisions are made by the community as a whole and not by individuals. To a Westerner, such family obligations may seem a burden, but in the primal society this is the very factor which gives value to the individual. People, therefore, live out their lives within the community. Thus, for example, an individual does not merely decide to go fishing on his own, because when he returns others will ask him to share his fish with them. He will be socially obliged to share what he has caught. The men will therefore only go fishing as a group and then all will have fish. Such group participation is also socially enjoyable.

This is an important point described by Donald McGavran as a 'People Movement'.[11] He describes how societies with a high people-consciousness are unlikely to make individualistic decisions to become Christian as is common in the West. They will discuss the matter between themselves and eventually come to a decision.

Age is important and respected. Old people are consulted over decisions because they have a wealth of experience. Parents in Western society are involved in making wedding arrangements, but it is rare for a son or daughter to ask their parents advice about a possible marriage partner. Western society places an emphasis upon knowledge and physical ability. This knowledge comes from schools and universities, and most parents are out of touch with latest technology. The Westerner therefore speaks of 'the generation gap'.

Time

To John Mbiti, time is the key to understanding the worldview of sub-Saharan Africa.[12] He insists that the Western linear concept of time with its indefinite past, a present, and an indefinite future is foreign to African thinking.

For the African, time has two dimensions. It has a past and a present, but virtually no future. Mbiti describes time as moving backwards rather than forward, with people focusing upon what has taken place rather than what they wish to occur in the future. It is like travelling on a train with one's back to the engine. One can see the space about the carriage, and the hills which have been passed, but the future is not perceived. 'This constitutes an indefinite "past" which is the terminus of all phenomena and events, and which is dominated by the myth: and an intensely active "present" in which the individual or community is most conscious of his (its) existence and being.'[13]

Time is not a valued commodity as in the West. People enjoy the company of others, and do not have the Western concern that they must 'get on with things'. Long-term planning is therefore often missing within primal societies as many development workers have discovered to their frustration.

Any fundamental change is viewed with suspicion, for such innovation might carry within them the seeds of retribution from the unseen powers. To launch out into the unknown is dangerous and might disturb the natural equilibrium. Thus, primal societies tend to follow the traditions of their ancestors. Human life follows a rhythm of natural phenomena like birth, procreation and death, or day and night, or the seasons of the year.

Value

Ethical values are related to the family or social group. As Louis Luzbetak states in his study of the Middle Wahgi worldview themes, 'The ultimate norm for "good" or "bad", "right" and "wrong" is the clan.'[14] It is the traditions which are passed on from the ancestors who have given a framework of what is considered to be 'good' and 'bad'.

The clan, or family, is always right. To disagree with the family is an act of betrayal. The ultimate punishment for disobedience to the family, or tribe, is expulsion from the community. Without social ties the person loses all value and becomes a non-person. 'Outsiders', on the other hand, are generally regarded as hostile, and have no rights. It is acceptable to steal from them, or injure them, provided no repercussions come upon the tribe.

The continuity of the family is all important. Thus, it is essential that every adult has children, and at least some of these children grow up to have children in their turn. The greatest curse that a woman can know is to be barren. It means that she and her husband will be the last link in the human chain. A man will therefore divorce a wife who is barren, or take a second wife. Family planning will not be considered until the couple have a minimum of five or six children, because only then can they be assured of one son who will grow up and have sons of his own.

Due to one's dependence upon one's ancestors, and the associated concept of their superiority, it means that the traditions passed down from these fore-fathers are 'good' and 'valuable'. Tradition is important and should be followed. A failure to do so will lead to problems. Don Richardson tells the story of a Yali girl from Irian Jaya who inadvertently wandered into a sacred garden. These gardens were taboo to women, and the punishment for such an act was death. Although in tears over the impending punishment, the girl's father handed the child over to his eldest son to throw her into the roaring river. If this punishment had not been carried out the whole cycle of nature would have been disrupted, and the whole family suffer.[15]

The concept of a universe penetrated by unseen powers allows for the possibility of certain people using these powers for their own advantage. Witchcraft and sorcery are considered to be the anti-social use of such powers to cause harm to some person or persons. On the other hand, there are other members of the community who may use their powers for the good of the community, such as witch-doctors, and healers. The evaluation of the ethics of the use is based upon the value it provides to the community, but in all cases the power is regarded with respect and even fear.

Conflict within primal worldviews

The primal worldview is adequate for a society which faces few changes. These are small societies where there is little by way of innovation. They are isolated both from ecological changes and contact with other cultures having different customs and ideas. Contact with a dominant foreign culture causes major trauma to the society. The traditions of the elders suddenly seem to become unreliable guides to the new situation, and the old worldview becomes questioned. The time-tested traditions that used to successfully account for experiences now seem to be irrelevant. The world seems to be falling apart.

It is for this reason that many primal societies have converted to one of the so-called 'world religions' such as Islam or Christianity. These world religions have endured long, and have spread so far precisely because the worldviews they carry are able to fit a wide variety of human experiences. World religions are either monotheistic, believing in one Creator God, or monistic, believing in one universal reality. In contrast, primal religions have a complex cosmology with many gods, spirits, ghosts, and devils, relating to one particular society. The tribal society is portrayed as if it is the only real people on earth, and their land the centre of the world. The unifying cosmological beliefs of a world religion lead to a unification of humanity which in turn makes the religion applicable to all, and thus it becomes a world religion.

Primal worldviews are basically fragile, and easily fracture in contact with larger societies, especially if the latter have a developed technology as most do. For this reason, world religions have grown essentially through the conversion of primal societies, and have had relatively little success in converting people who already have an allegiance to another world religion. Christianity, for example, grew in the first, second and third centuries by the conversion of the primal societies of the Mediterranean region. In the fourth and fifth centuries, growth occurred in the north of Europe amongst the Celtic and Saxon people. With the rapid expansion of Islam in the seventh century, the growth of Christianity was halted until the eighteenth and nineteenth centuries when the Christianised European peoples made contact with primal societies in Africa, Asia and Latin America.

It is rare for people to shift in their thinking from one set of assumptions to another over-night. Usually, one or two major themes from the new worldview are accepted as more reasonable answers to the questions people are faced with. As the people learn more about the new worldview, they seek to rationalise the new ideas in terms of their traditional thought patterns. They may therefore arrive at a somewhat distorted, or mixed, view of the new religion and its accompanying worldview. This process of syncretism is one in which two, or more, differing sets of belief and practice are modified and accommodated to each other to produce what is essentially a new system.

A polytheistic cosmology is more amenable to syncretism than other worldviews by virtue of the fact that the new gods can be introduced into the traditional pantheon. People may thus call themselves Hindus, Muslims or Christians, but they retain much of their traditional worldview. This 'folk' aspect of a world religion results from a lack of education in the new religion, and so is common amongst the poor. Because they are untaught in the great philosophies and theologies, they retain the ancient beliefs and fashion for themselves superstitions and rituals to deal with contemporary stresses and crises.

Another way in which a society may respond to the pressures of a dominant worldview, and rapidly changing culture is the process that anthropologists call 'revitalisation'.[16] From out of the mixture of traditional and new beliefs emerges a totally new explanation of reality. This revitalisation of society comes from a conscious, deliberate and organised attempt by some person, or persons within a society, to create a more satisfying culture. Thus primal religions with their characteristic worldviews should not be regarded as some ancient fossils from the past confined to the history books. Primal religions have a way of emerging from within world religions in new fashions, to capture the imaginations of a contemporary generation attracted by the novelty of the ancient.

Notes

1. Beals, Alan R. *Culture in Process* (Holt, Reinhart & Winston: New York, 1979) p 241.
2. Turner, Harold W. *Living Tribal Religions* (Ward Lock Educa-

tional: London, 1974), p 7.

3. Neill, Stephen *Christian Faith and Other Faiths* (Oxford University Press: Oxford, 1970) p 125.
4. Rubingh, Eugene. *Sons of Tiv* (Baker Book House: Grand Rapids, 1969) pp 71–72.
5. Hart, C.W.M. and Pilling, Arnold. *The Tiwi of North Australia* (Holt, Reinhart & Winston: New York, 1960).
6. Kirby, Jon P. 'Bush Fires and the Domestication of the Wild in Ghana' in *Occasional Papers, Culture and Development*, series No 1, April 1987.
7. Burnett, David. *Unearthly Powers* (Monarch: Eastbourne, 1988) p 49.
8. Burnett, *ibid*.
9. Mbiti, John S. *New Testament Eschatology in an Afircan Background* (SPCK: London, 1978) p 10.
10. Burnett, *op cit*, pp 19–20.
11. McGavran, Donald. *Bridges of God* (World Dominion Press: London, 1955). See also Donald McGavran, *Understanding Church Growth* (Eerdmans Pub: Grand Rapids, 1970) pp 296–314.
12. Mbiti, *op cit*, p 24.
13. Mbiti, *ibid*, p 30.
14. Luzbetak, Louis J. *The Church and Cultures* (Divine Word Publication: Techny, 1970) p 164.
15. Richardson, Don. *Lords of the Earth* (G L Regal: Glendale, 1977).
16. Wallace, Anthony F.C. *Religion: An Anthropological View* (Random House: New York, 1966).

5

GODS AND GURUS:
The Hindu Worldview

Hinduism is a very ancient religion which has flourished like an over-grown plant, originating from the primal worldview of the societies of the Indian sub-continent. Unlike the more recent world religions such as Christianity and Islam, Hinduism is essentially the faith of a single cultural unit, the Hindus, in the same way as Judaism is the religion of the Jews. Its very variety and synthesis has encouraged it to thrive and spread into many societies.

The beginnings of Hindu philosophy are to be found some 6,000 years ago when there emerged a distinctive system of beliefs about the cosmos. The early philosophers framed a system of belief based on the acceptance of one indescribable force, impersonal, and without any attributes – 'Brahman'. This key paradigm constructs a monistic worldview with endless repercussions that result in philosophies vastly different from those common in the West.

These ideas were written down in a complex body of literature known as the *Vedas*, written between 1000 BC and AD 500. The *Vedas*, from the word 'veda' meaning 'knowledge', form the supreme authority for Hindus. The most important section, called the *Upanishads*, deals with such fundamental questions as the meaning of life and the nature of the universe. Living beings are seen as having an endless series of lives achieved through a continual process of reincarnations into which all are locked until they can be freed through enlightenment. Only then can one be unfettered from the cycle of life and death, and ascend into higher planes of existence outside the reach of space and time.

Hinduism has no single founder like Christianity or Islam. It does not have an established creed, or body of doctrine. Hinduism is like an exotic plant with many and varied blooms. It is not one system of beliefs, but a series of inter-related ideas. Raymond Hammer described Hinduism in the following way:

> Hinduism has no founder and no prophet. It has no particular ecclesiastical or institutional structure, nor set creed. The emphasis is on the way of living rather than on a way of thought. Radhakrishnan, a former president of India, once remarked: 'Hinduism is more a culture than a creed.'[1]

The distinction between the level of popular belief and that of the elaborate rituals and philosophies is very marked. In the villages of India one finds concepts, and practices very similar to those described under the term 'primal worldview', with the addition of Hindu names for some of the gods. In this present chapter, the aim is to consider the major themes of the Hindu worldview whilst all the time recognising the great variety of local expressions which it may take.

Hindu worldview themes

English fails to provide the words to explain many of the complex concepts of Hindu philosphy. It is therefore necessary to use many Sanskrit words to convey, at least in part, the meaning of these perceptions. This fact provides an illustration of the great differences which exist between Western and Hindu philosophy.

The Cosmos

There is a well known story of three men disputing the correct description of an elephant which they had never seen. Each in turn went into a darkened room which contained an elephant. The first man went into the room, groped around and eventually touched the leg of the elephant. He emerged saying that an elephant was like a tree. The second man entered, and felt the trunk of the elephant. He emerged saying that the elephant was like a snake. The third man entered and bumped into the side of the elephant, and concluded that the elephant was like a wall. Which man is right? All the men have mistaken the little they have touched for the true and complete reality.

The perception that physical phenomena are real is called *maya* by Hindus. It is as if the universal reality were playing tricks upon us, making each of us believe that our bodies, this book, the chair are real. They are in fact illusion. The answer to the schoolboy question, 'Does the world really exist or is it merely a projection in my own mind?' seems like a joke to the secular worldview, but emphasises the truth of the Hindu concept of *maya*.

In the concept *maya*, the world we perceive is no more than a creation of our own minds. The 'really real' is behind or beyond the world of sensory experience. One must go past the material forms to the one divine mystery that envelops and manifests itself as all the little objects which I regard as realities. There is only one true reality. The ultimate reality is 'Brahman', the one, infinite impersonal existence. Brahman is all that exists, and anything else which appears to exist is *maya*, and does not truly exist at all. Ultimate reality is beyond distinction, it merely is. There is therefore a unity of all things. All things are manifestations of the one 'Brahman'.

There is therefore no distinction between objective experiences and illusion and dream. Fact and fantasy merge into one. The subjective imaginations of the mind are as much a part of a person's experimental world as are his 'awake' experiences. There is no distinction between what the Westerner would call 'supernatural' and 'natural'. Gods and spirits, demons and ghosts blend with the natural realm to make a single system. The universe is unpredictable, and things are not what they first appear to be. In sharp contrast with the secular worldview, unpredictable changes are always taking place. Demons may take the form of beautiful maidens, and gods the form of beggars.

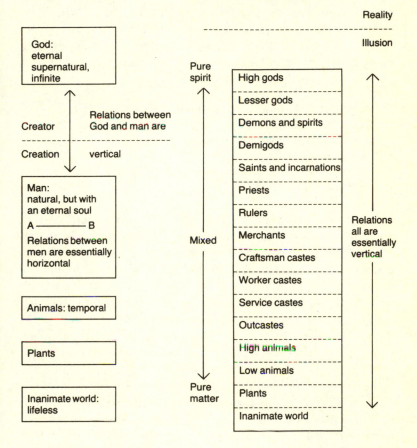

Figure 5.1. Comparison of American and Indian views of life.

The cosmos is presided over by a High God, on whom it depends, and is governed with the aid of many lesser gods. Hinduism is basically monotheistic, but devotees are divided into three broad groups according to the nature of this deity. Some worship deity as Vishnu, others Siva, and others Sakti, who is conceived of as the female aspect of Siva. Even though these deities are recognised, they are not seen as exclusive, but merely different ways of looking at the same god. The monotheism of Islam, Judaism and Christianity has arisen from an exclusion of other deities, whilst Hinduism has assimilated many gods. The actual focus of worship is therefore not of such importance as is the reverence itself.

> Whatever celestial form a devotee (craving for some worldly object) seeks to worship with faith, I stabilise the faith of that particular devotee in that very form.
> Endowed with such faith he worships that deity and obtains through him without doubt his desired enjoyment as ordained by Me. *Bhagavadgita* 7:21,22.

This notion of synthesis is a major distinction between Western and Hindu philosophy. Western philosophy is basically analytical, whilst synthesis has been called 'the genius of Hindu thought'.[2] This is illustrated in that the concepts of the phenomenal world are not divided into distinct classes, as in the secular worldview, but as a continuum. It is like a ladder with many rungs along which are found an infinite variety of beings: gods, demons, people, animals, plants, and insects (see Figure 5:1). Life itself is, however, one.

The Self

From the times of the earliest *Upanishads*, written about 600 BC, the theme of the unity of the individual soul with the supreme reality has been accepted. Human beings, and that which they would each call 'I' are just as unsubstantial as the external world. Individuality and human consciousness is just a part of the total illusion of *maya*. The individual soul, *atman*, is in fact the divine self which is identical with 'Brahman'. Thus, ultimate reality lies within, rather than without. The focus of human achievement therefore becomes world-denying, rather than world-affirming as with the secular worldview.

To realise one's true oneness with the cosmos is to pass beyond personality. It is the awareness of personality which inhibits and binds one to the sense of illusion. The merging with 'Brahman', the only reality, is the way of release. The Hindu concept is therefore totally different from theism which stresses the reality of human personality. Personality demands self-consciousness which requires a distinction between the thinker and the thing thought about.

That which binds man to the illusion of the material universe is *karma*. Each self (*atman*) goes through a series of births and rebirths which, in the manner of the phenomenal world, is almost endless. Death is not the end, but merely a stage on the endless cycle of birth-and-rebirth, *samsara*. *Karma* is the law which determines the form in which one will be born in the next existence. If one has lived a good life, one builds up good *karma* and will be born in a higher station, or to a happier life. Good and bad are built up over the reincarnations, the balance being passed on to future lives.

Karma will affect the form into which you are born in ensuing lives. Hinduism maintains that all living things have souls, which are essentially equal, and are only distinguished through *karma*. *Karma* helps to explain the seeming unfairness of life. Why does someone become ill? Why does a woman win a lottery? Why did an accident occur? Bad *karma* from a previous life may provide at least part of an answer.

If living creatures are locked into what is an endless cycle of births and rebirths which seems to go on for a monotonous eternity, what is the purpose? There must be a way of release from the bonds of earthly existence. The desire for release, known as *moksha*, has lead many thoughtful men to press beyond the limits of experience to find reality.

Knowing

Wisdom (*jnana*) is the ultimate goal for humanity. Unlike

knowledge which comes by rational analysis and often has little influence upon his actual behaviour, wisdom comes as a flash of inner light with insights which transform a person's life and relationships. The wise come to realise that the world is *maya*, and their best attitude to this is that of passivity and non-attach-ment.

Western philosophy has focused upon analytical thinking in which a topic is broken down into component parts. This is exactly the approach which we are using in this present text. Hindu philosophy, on the other hand, is concerned with mysti-cal insight which by definition is beyond the description of rational analysis. Mysticism uses the language of symbols and analogies. Hindus, therefore, make use of sacred sounds to open new states of transcendental experience and knowledge. These sounds, or *mantra* are one-word spells, such as 'hum', 'hrim', and 'klam', and are often the name of some Hindu deity. In the holy city of Benares, devotees may come to spend twenty-four hours repeating the name 'Ram'.

Community

The concept of all things being part of a continuum expresses itself in the hierarchical nature within human society. The caste system is only part of a larger social order which extends from gods and spirits to plants and insects. Each person has a unique place in this order as a result of the *karma* from previous lives. Thus people are not of equal value, but are ranked within a mul-tiple caste system (Figure 5.1).[3] Each caste has its own skills and specialised functions. A person is born into a particular caste and as such, his life-style, occupation, and even the food he eats are designated. There is no possibility of social mobility.

Diversity and cooperation within a community are the emphasised ideas rather than competition. Some people are born to greater rights and responsibilities than others which results in a hierarchy of human relations. In this hierarchy some individuals are dependent upon others for particular favours, and they in turn show loyalty to their superiors. This is usually known by anthropologists as the patron-client relationship.

The cultural pluralism and mutual cooperation which results from the caste system, leads to a spirit of tolerance of others. People do not seek to convert others to their own particular way of life. A person's primary social ties are with his own caste, or *jati* (sub-caste). A person must support the caste and follow its dictates.

Time

From Brahman, the supreme reality, all has come and all must return. Time is cyclic, an endless series of evolvings and devolvings. The universe is in a series of perpetual cycles of growth and decay said to be connected with the life of the god Vishnu. The basic cycle is the *kalpa*, the 'Day of Brahma', lasting 4,200 million earth years. According to Hindu mythology, the cosmic cycle begins with Vishnu asleep upon the enormous thousand-headed cobra Sesha. From Vishnu's navel slowly grows a lotus, and from the unfolding petals of the lotus is born the god Brahma. It is Brahma who creates the cosmos, after which Vishnu awakes and governs developments during the day, until once more Vishnu sleeps, and the cosmos is absorbed into his body. The cosmic night lasts as long as the day. Vishnu is now said to be in his fifty-first year. When a hundred years are completed, Vishnu, and the cosmos contained within him, will merge with Brahman, the Absolute Reality. Ultimately Brahman will once more develop a personality, a new Vishnu will be born, and the process repeated.

Within the basic cycle, the *kalpa*, are lesser cycles, the most important of which are the great aeons, or *mahayugas*. There are 1,000 of these in every *kalpa*, each divided into four aeons. We are presently believed to be in the period of the *kali-yuga*, which began in 3102 BC, and will come to an end after 432,000 years due to fire and flood.

The cyclic notion of time comes through into the understanding of an individual's existence. Everybody is believed to be reborn thousands of times through a multitude of levels and castes. In practice, the value of an individual life becomes diminished. A Hindu mother consoles herself over the death of her baby by saying, 'Never mind, there are many babies.' What does it matter if a beggar dies on the street? He may be reincarnated into a better form.

Value

If there is but one ultimate reality, it means that the cosmos must be perfect at every moment. Consequently, there is no absolute morality. This does not mean that Hindu philosophers would deny morality, but stress the pursuit of the 'Three Aims' – religious merit, wealth and pleasure. The first should override the second, and the claims of both, the third.

It has already been mentioned that *karma* is the concept that one's present state, be it happy or sad, rich or poorer, is the result of past actions, especially in former existences. In its progress back to Brahman the *atman* goes through an endless series of illusory forms dependent upon past actions. One reaps what one sows. Living, for the Hindu, can be seen as an attempt to build up good *karma*.

One builds up good *karma* not by 'doing good' actions like helping old ladies cross the street, but by doing one's duty and living within the rules of his particular caste. A son must obey his father. A wife must obey her husband and treat him with reverence. A man of the sweeper caste must perform his task of being a sweeper. Each person has a *dharma* determined in part by his position in the family, his caste and his age. Each person must be faithful to obey their *dharma*. 'Right' is conformity to the cosmic order.

> One's own duty, though devoid of merit, is preferable to the duty of another well performed. Even death in the performance of one's own duty brings blessedness; another's duty is fraught with fear. *Bhagavadgita* 3:35.

This leads to the notion of passivity and non-violence. The aim of caste law is not justice in absolute terms, but the restoration of harmony within the social group. Actions cannot be divided into good and evil, nor people into offender and the offended.

Man cannot punish actions whose cause he can never fully understand, and must leave final justice to the law of *karma*.

The goal in life therefore is not self-actualisation, as in secular worldviews, but release from the hardships of *karma*. This process is usually called *moksha*, and requires the use of techniques known as *yoga*. The cultural hero of the Hindu worldview is the man who gains wisdom and is able to dissociate himself from the desire for material things and sensual pleasure. Thus, in Hinduism, the holiest of men are both poor and naked. They have come to the point of denying their desire for material needs. They are homeless religious beggars, wandering the length and breadth of the land, owning nothing and attached to nothing. When they gather for the great annual festivals, even the footprints which they leave in the ground are considered holy. Lesser mortals grovel on the floor to touch the imprints of these most holy of people.

These worldview themes seem 'unbelievable' to those from a Judeo-Christian tradition. This is perhaps why relatively few Hindus have in fact been converted to Christianity. The two worldviews seem so totally different that they are almost incomprehensible to each other. Even so, the influence of Western technology has continued in India, but what may be more surprising is the growing influence of the Hindu worldview themes within Western society. To follow this development one needs to look further at the ideas of *yoga*.

Yoga

Enlightenment can be achieved by many paths generally called *yoga*. The word *yoga* comes from the Sanskrit root *yuj*, which means *to unite*. It has the connotation both of submission to discipline and of union. Probably *spiritual discipline* is the best translation of the term.

It was Patanjali, who, in about 300 BC, wrote the Yoga Sutras in which he taught that eight disciplines were necessary in yoga:

1 Yama –   restraint, abstention from harming others.

2   Niyama –   observance, physical & mental purity.
3   Asana –   physical exercise.
4   Pranayama – breath control to gain mastery of vital energy.
5   Pratyahara – withdrawal, detachment from sensuality.
6   Dharana – concentration, fixing the mind on a single point.
7   Dhyana – meditation.
8   Samadhi – self-collectedness, being able to see the object of concentration as it really is.[4]

These 'eight limbs' still form the framework for most yoga systems today. By themselves they form a system known as Raja yoga. Apart from the introductory ideas in stage three, Asana, the system bears little resemblance to what most Western people currently think of as yoga with its posture exercises. This did not emerge until the fifteenth century, with a form of yoga known as *Hatha*.

There are six major yoga systems.

1)   *Hatha – yoga of bodily control*

The word *Hatha* (pronounced *hat-ha*) is made up of the syllable *ha*, meaning moon, and *tha*, which means sun. The reason for this is that yogis believe that there are two warring impulses, set in motion every time we breathe. The moon impulse (*prana vayu*) begins in the heart and ascends up to the brain. The sun impulse (*apana vayu*) starts at the solar plexus and heads downwards to the anus. The discord between these contrary pulls causes the restlessness we experience in mind and body.

Hatha yoga tries to harness these two sets of currents, and by making them unite to still both body and mind. The person would then be free to concentrate upon one's true 'Self'. The breathing exercises are all designed to create the uniting of these two currents. What should then happen is that the concentration of energy is pushed down to the base of the spine. Here there is situated one of the seven *chakras* (spiritual energy centres) of the body, and also the entrance to the *sushumna*, the central spinal canal (see Figure 5.2).

For most people, the *sushumna* is never opened, as long as they live. On the other hand, the yogi manages to push energy through the *sushumna*, and he suddenly finds that spiritual life has become all at once much easier. Not only may he go directly to Patanjali's stages six, seven and eight, but a wide range of spiritual options open themselves to him.

This, then, is what the physical exercises of yoga are really for. Any benefits to physical fitness are merely secondary. The British Wheel of Yoga concentrates heavily upon Hatha. However, many yogi regard Hatha as merely the preliminary exercises to be gone through before real yoga begins.

2)   *Jnana – Yoga of knowledge*

Jnana yoga is the yoga of wisdom, and is composed of mental effort. It is often thought suitable for people of an intellectual type of mind. It involves meditation upon the Vedic scriptures, and thoughtful discernment of all the circumstances of life. The ordinary reasoning mind cannot achieve this, and so an intense state of frustration results. At this point of absolute despair the true Self will reveal itself, and the person will jettison the logical mind in favour of direct experience.

3)   *Karma – Yoga of action*

Karma yoga is the yoga of work and everyday life. In a poem of a conversation between Krishna and the warrior Arjuna, Krishna reveals to him that work can be worship.

> Do your allotted work, for action is superior to nonaction. Even the normal functions of your body cannot be accomplished through actionlessness.
>
> Except for the action done for sacrifice, all men are under bondage of action (karma). Therefore, Arjuna, do you undertake action for that purpose, becoming free from all attachment. *Bhagavadgita* 3:8,9.

Figure 5.2
Kundalini Yoga's view of the psychic centres of the body

The logic of Karma yoga is as follows. All people must act, but the wise man acts in a detached manner without 'self' involvement. The actions are therefore no longer his actions since they are not performed for self-gratification. The process of karma is thus terminated, and the man is free. The principle is inaction in action.

The best-known karma yogi was probably Mahatma Gandhi, a man capable of an incredible work rate. Sri Aurobindo was probably the most influential writer of this school. He has only a few followers in Britain.

4) *Bhakti – Yoga of devotion*

The best-known Hindu cult is that of the Bhakti form. The Hara Krishna people dressed in their exotic saffron robes are a familiar sight in many high streets.

Bhakti means 'devotion'. In this form of yoga, the adherent is supposed to achieve union with the ultimate reality by giving his love and worship unremittingly to one of the personal forms of God. Hindus believe that although Brahman is impersonal, he/it may be worshipped as a person. One way of devoting oneself is to repeatedly chant the sacred form of words. Sacred word forms are called *mantra*, and the most popular is that of the Maha mantra, or 'Great Hymn'.

> Hara Krishna, Hara Krishna,
> Krishna Krishna, Hara Hara,
> Hara Rama, Hara Rama,
> Rama Rama, Hara Hara.

By incessant chanting it is believed that one loses attachment to material things, and is drawn away from the fascinations of *maya*, to fall in love with reality itself.

So far, we have looked at four classical forms of yoga. Two other systems of yoga have emerged: Tantric and Kundalini. There has often been mixed views with regards to the potential of developing para-normal abilities within yoga. TM, for example, asserts that it can teach people to levitate. Other yogi have stressed the dangers of seeking such phenomena.

5) *Kundalini*

The first of the two major forms of yoga associated with the paranormal is *Kundalini*. Kundalini is the word used to describe the powerful energy force reckoned to lie, coiled and dormant, at the base of the spine (see Figure 5.2). Kundalini yoga involves various techniques for awakening the energy force and making it arise slowly up the spinal column. As it rises, it passes through each of the *chakras* (the seven psychic centres of the human body), and as it contacts each, various psychic experiences take place. When the practitioner becomes skilled enough to raise the kundalini to the utmost *chakra*, he receives the ability to perform miracles and gain liberation from *maya*. Patanjali had briefly mentioned the possibility of yoga developing para-normal abilities. He had not been interested in these, and viewed them as a mere by-product. Kundalini can be dangerous, and many Hatha yogi warn against its practice.

6) *Tantrism*

Most forms of yoga involve discipline, but the Tantric texts suggested the possibility of using some of the natural impulses of the body in yoga rather than suppressing them. Sex, especially, was seen as a possible route to reality. Prolonging the sexual act, it was claimed, generates a flow of sexual energy between the two partners so that both begin to experience the ultimate Oneness of reality.

6   Most orthodox Hindus were scandalised by these ideas. Patanjali had in general ignored bodily processes, and especially sexual intercourse. Frequent sexual intercourse he regarded as resulting in a loss of spiritual power. The Hatha form of yoga was probably stimulated as a counter-action to Tantrism which made prolonged sexual intercourse a route to enlightenment.

Tantrism has had an impact both on Hinduism and Buddhism, especially in Tibet. Perhaps it is not surprising that Tantric yoga with its emphasis upon sex has interested many in the Western world. The most well-known exponent, Bhagwan Shree Rajneesh, has attracted publicity by his flamboyant lifestyle. When someone joins the movement, they are given a new name, required to wear orange clothes, and carry a picture of Rajneesh. Apart from that, rules are at a minimum. They are free sexually, and indulge in meditation which involves violent movement, chaotic breathing and shaking of the body to produce a state of euphoria. We shall return to the growth of these movements in a later chapter.

Developments within Hinduism

The nineteenth-century European was shocked and disgusted by much of Hindu culture. The blatant idolatry, animal sacrifice, child marriage and untouchability appeared primitive in his Western eyes. He had an air of confidence about the superiority of his own culture and religion.

> A hundred years ago, at the time of the Mutiny, there were many missionaries in India who sincerely believed that within a few generations the whole of India would become Christian. The oppressive system of ceremonial restrictions and taboos, which was the most obvious aspect of Hinduism to one who did not look below the surface, seemed bound to perish in the face of such Western innovations as railways, scientific medicine and widespread literacy, leaving a gap which could only be filled by the religion of Christ.[5]

However, the European was soon to discover that beneath the outward practices lay a philosophy richer than he could imagine. The 'gap' which resulted from contact with Western civilisation was to be filled by new developments within Hinduism itself. A worldview which has survived for centuries must have great resilience, and Hinduism has an amazing potential to assimilate rather than exclude. Over the last century, Hinduism has quietly shed much of its outward rituals and ceremonies, and adapted itself to the conditions of the twentieth century. Much of ancient Hinduism is still to be found in the villages of India, but this is giving way to the new, not by some religious revolution, but by a steady process of adaption.

The ideas of the Hindu worldview were to be released into the West with Max Muller's great series on *The Sacred Books of the East*, the first volume of which was published in 1875. The depth of philosophical thought came as something of a shock to the European who had become gradually more enthralled with this worldview so different from his own.

Christians have entered into an uneasy dialogue with Hindus. This is not a matter of debating which is the superior of two different religious traditions, but an interaction between two totally different sets of paradigms. Christians have therefore responded in various and often conflicting ways. This is illustrated, for example, in the variety of Christian opinions concerning yoga. As we have already seen, yoga is an essential mechanism for spiritual release within Hinduism, and is thus a vital component within the practice of this religion.

There are four main attitudes that have been taken by Christians with regards to yoga.

1)   The initial reaction of most Christians has been that yoga is demonic, and can have an evil influence. Certain types of yoga, such as Tantric and Kundalini, do involve para-normal phenomena, and may cause such harmful effects. However, one has to then ask, what about Hatha yoga? May this be used as a spiritual exercise within any religion?

2)   Some have argued that all religions, by the very fact that they are religious, are essentially Bhakti yoga. However, this is to use the word 'yoga' so widely that it hardly means anything of distinction. There is certainly an element of mysticism found in any religious experience, but this is not the same as what is understood by 'yoga'.

3)   Yoga is considered to be an applied philosophy and not a

religious system. Yoga and religion are different, and are complementary like science and literature. There is nothing that TM sympathisers insist upon more strongly than that TM is a neutral technique. They claim that it is an objective device for relieving stress and achieving relaxation. Thus, they would claim, Christians may use yoga as a 'natural' way to relax, and keep healthy.

Why does TM so strongly deny this religious involvement? John Allan argues that this is because, 'the facade of science and therapy is no more than a "come-on" for the real Hindu message. (As Maharishi himself noted, "If TM were a religion, it would be meaningful only to a small segment of the world").... After initiation, a great deal of pressure can be put upon the new meditator to get "more involved", to go on weekend retreats, to advance to the stage of "checker" by helping out at the local TM centre, then to become a teacher oneself, and even after that to undergo advanced courses, involving more and more occultist and oriental assumptions.'[6] If Allan is correct one can see that TM provides a facade for Hinduism which would be culturally relevant to the secular Western world.

4)   Following on from views two and three, some Christians have argued that yoga might be Christianised. It would then become simply a preparation for communion with God, an emptying of oneself in order to appreciate more fully the grace of God. Jean-Marie Dechanet has been a major exponent of this position in his book *Christian Yoga* which is mostly concerned with Hatha yoga.[7] However, Hatha yoga was not developed to stand on its own, but as a preparation for Raja yoga. How can it therefore be in any way used for truly Christian purposes when yoga is so firmly based upon Hindu paradigms?

The Hindu worldview has an amazing plasticity which allows it to adapt to new situations, and yet remain true to its ancient assumptions. The ability to synthesise, and allow individual variety and creativity, will allow Hinduism a place even within Western society. The growing attraction of the New Age movement is one expression of the virility of this ancient religion.

Notes

1. Hammer, Raymond. 'The Eternal Teaching: Hinduism' in *The World Religions* (Lion: Tring, 1982) p 170.
2. Zaehner, R.C. *Encyclopedia of Living Faiths* (Hutchinson: London, 1988) p 225.
3. Hiebert, Paul G. *Cultural Anthropology* (Lippincott: Philadelphia, 1976) p 36.
4. Allan, John. *Yoga* (IVP: Leicester, 1983) p 15.
5. Zaehner, R.C. *op cit*, p 253.
6. Allan, John. *TM: A Cosmic Confidence Trick* (IVP: Leicester, 1980) p 30.
7. Dechanet, Jean-Marie. *Christian Yoga* (Search Press: Tunbridge Wells, 1984).

6

ANCESTORS AND ALMANACS:
The Chinese Worldview

Approximately one out of every five persons on the face of the earth is Chinese. They represent what is clearly the longest surviving, and richest of civilisations. As such, one would expect them to have one of the most resilient and practical of worldviews. With all the great movements which have occurred amongst the Chinese this century, it is impossible to identify a prevailing Chinese worldview, but it is possible to describe something of the traditional worldview.

The people of present day China may be divided into two, the Han Chinese, and the ethnic minorities in Outer and Inner China who make up only 6% of the population. The origins of the Han Chinese are still undetermined. It is unlikely that they were of one original race, but consisted of many separate centres of civilisation. The Chou dynasty is one of the oldest known in China (1122–221 BC). This period saw the painful birth of a unified China after much bloodshed and warfare.

The Han dynasty was founded by Liu Pang who assumed the title of Emperor in 202 BC. The dynasty lasted some 400 years and developed a social and legal structure which was to influence the following generations of Chinese. The Han period was one of major cultural attainment and scientific discovery. However, by the end of the second century AD, the Han Empire had virtually ceased to exist, and it fragmented into three kingdoms.

The social and political upheaval of this period was accompanied by intense intellectual activity. During most of the Han period, Confucianism, as the official ideology, had provided the government with a standard code of morals. Confucianism is not a body of ideas to which an unbeliever can be converted, but a way of life which could only be practised within traditional Chinese society. Confucianism is now dead within China, but its influence upon the Chinese worldview remains strong to this day.

Taoism was another philosophy which grew during the period of the Chou and Han Empires. The legendary founder of Taoism was Lao-tzu, the 'Old Fellow', who was born in 604 BC according to tradition. The basic concepts of the Tao stem from the primal religions which flourished earlier in Chinese history, and provided a second stream to Chinese thought.

A third stream of influence was to come from India with Buddhist missionaries. The large scale development of Chinese Buddhism started only after the barbarian invasions of the early fourth century. Up until then, Buddhism was largely the religion of foreigners. The new religion interacted with Chinese thought to form a particularly Chinese expression. This was especially accepted among the ruling classes, and Emperor Wu (reigned AD 502–546) became one of its earliest patrons. Among the many ordinary people there was clearly much mixing of Buddhism, Taoism, and traditional religious ideas.

The ensuing history of China is one of the fragmentation of the land into numerous smaller kingdoms during the period up to the establishment of the Sung dynasty (AD 960). The northern and southern Sung pledged peaceful coexistence which produced a flowering of civilization. The institutional framework which evolved during the Sung period remained unchanged until the nineteenth century.

The Sung Empire was eventually to fall to the invasion of the Mongols (1276). The Mongols did not try to impose their own religion (Shamanism) on their subjects. This gave comparative freedom for the existing religions to flourish. However, rivalries amongst the Mongol generals weakened the government, and lead to insurrections. Finally Chu Yuan-chang established, in AD 1368, what was to become the Ming dynasty. As before, the establishment of a state government was to lead to a renewal of civilisation and culture. Fine art and literature developed.

During the Ming dynasty there came a major synthesis of the three great religions through religious thinkers such as Lin Chao-en (1517–98). He sought to harmonise the three religions into one by drawing upon the best elements of Taoism, Confucianism and Buddhism. The synthesis was so effectual that no Chinese would think it strange to be concurrently Buddhist, Confucianist and Taoist.

The Manchus were the descendants of the Juchen tribes of Manchuria who had founded the Chin dynasty in the eleventh century. The growing influence of the Manchus eventually established the Ching dynasty which was eventually to lead to 100 years of domestic peace in the late seventeenth century and eighteenth century. It was after this time that the Chinese people were to begin to feel the increasing influence of the European peoples. From the West came the Russians, and by sea the British, Dutch, and German. These nations were drawn by the economic wealth of the most populous nation on earth.

Contact with European nations added yet another element to the modern Chinese worldview. The Chinese are assimilating a new cultural perspective as they did with Buddhism 1,800 years ago.

> The worldview of multiplied millions of Chinese over a period of two and one-half millennia has been fashioned out of tribal religion, the philosophies of the two great Chinese masters, and, subsequently, by the tendency to integrate the various elements into a religious but practical worldview.[1]

Chinese worldview themes

The Cosmos

The core of Chinese traditional belief is that the world of man and the world of nature are inseparable and interdependent. As Rev E.J.Eitel wrote in 1873, '(The Chinese) look upon nature not as a dead inanimate fabric, but as a living breathing organism. They see a golden chain of spiritual life running every form of existence and binding together, as in one living body, everything that subsists on heaven above or on earth below.'[2]

The Westerner, with his secular worldview, tends to regard the physical world as something 'out there', often as a hostile environment, whilst the Chinese sense the wholeness of the universe of which man is a part. This naturalistic philosophy is not without order because the Chinese conceive of an absolute which many translators have felt is best left in its transliterated form – Tao. Tao, literally means a road, or way, but in a wider connotation it means law, truth and order. Tao is the path which the universe follows, and all things evolve from that. Words cannot describe Tao. Tao is at once immanent and transcendent; it includes and pervades all that exists. Tao is change, process, the eternal states of being and non-being. This is a monism, not with a creator or a mind, but with a cosmic principle.

Tao manifests itself in the dual principles of 'yin' and 'yang'. This bipolarity of nature does not mean that everything simply has its opposite, but that opposites are necessary and complementary to each other. Yin and yang are diametrically opposed in character, and yet are equally essential for the existence of the universe. Associated with yang are the positive elements, such as heaven, light, heat, masculinity, life and strength. Yin includes the opposite elements: earth, darkness, cold, femininity, death and weakness.

This bi-polar principle was a very fruitful one as it allowed sense to be made out of the multitude of diverse facts in the universe. Out of the alternate actions of yin and yang are believed to develop the five primary elements (*hsing*) of fire, water, earth, wood, and metal. These elements are not static but are ceaselessly interacting and transforming each other. It was perhaps this aspect which allowed the development of a rich civilisation from the roots of a primal worldview.

One does not find the concept of a supreme Creator God

which is common to most primal societies, and, of course, to Western monotheism. The metaphysical concept of Tao may have been adequate for a few educated elite, but for the majority of people the forces of nature were personified as heavenly beings. The universe was seen as swarming with spirits, good (*shen*) and bad (*kwei*), ghosts and ancestors. These spirits control all parts of nature, and may bring blessing or harm upon human beings. It becomes necessary to do nothing to disturb these unseen powers, and for this reason the Chinese have a very practical view of the spirits and ancestors.

Amongst the multitude of deities the most popular is undoubtedly Kuan-yin, the goddess of mercy. Originally Kuan-yin was a bodhisattva called in the Indian Buddhist text Avalokitesvara. Although Kuan-yin is one of the major figures found in purely Buddhist temples she was adopted into popular folk belief and transformed into a compassionate mother figure. Thus, in popular religion she is the embodiment of loving kindness, giver of male children and helper in time of need.

The Self

The Chinese concept of the soul is not one which is clearly formulated, but must be gleaned from ideas of various teachers. Human beings, like every other thing in the universe, are a product of the interaction of yin and yang. This is most obviously seen through the new life which is produced through the uniting of male and female. Although there is such a dualism within the human constitution, it is not the same as that of body-and-soul known in the West, but a homogeneous mixing of the two. At death, the two components separate into the coarser and purer elements. Another way in which this has been conceived is that the human body is seen as being possessed by two souls, a superior spirit (*hun*, or *shen*), and an inferior or animal controller known as the *p'o*.[3] The *hun* takes possession of the child at birth, before which the *p'o* is in possession.

As with the primal worldview, it is believed that the soul may leave the body. When dreaming, for example, the *hun* may leave the body, and wander abroad. During these excursions its adventures are regarded as real happenings. The soul when separated from the body may be captured, or so terrified that it is unable to return. In this case the inferior soul assumes control and the man loses his reason.

Health is regarded as a state of balance between the body and the natural world as well as of balance between different components of the body itself. The five elements are linked to various organs of the body. As the five elements are linked to yin and yang, it is understandable that curing illness must be linked to the five elements (see Figure 6.1).[4]

Figure 6.1 Taoist Healing Methods

Elements	Yang Organs	Yin Organs	Cures
Fire	Small intestine	Heart	Spiritual cures
Wood	Gall bladder	Liver	Natural diet
Earth	Stomach	Spleen	Herbal therapy
Metal	Large intestine	Lungs	Acupuncture
Water	Urinary bladder	Kidneys	Thermogenesis

Sickness is caused by an excess of 'yang' or of 'yin' which affects the vital energy of the body, *chi*. A doctor will administer various cures to restore the balance to the *chi*.[5] Chi is believed to flow through the body along certain meridians, and it is into these that the acupuncturist will insert needles to reach various centres. Even the Chinese do not have a full explanation for the effectiveness of acupuncture, but it is considered to restore the body's balance by stimulating or retarding the body's forces.

At death, the *hun* escapes through the orifice at the top of the cranium, but the *p'o* remains until decomposition sets in. Depending upon the energy of the *p'o*, the body may possess frightening powers, and commit many kinds of atrocities. Thus, mortal remains are feared, the corpse is placed in a massive coffin, and even then treated with great care. However, if the deceased are properly interred, the *p'o* will rest peacefully, while the *hun* will send blessings to the surviving family members. As Laurence Thompson has expressed this: 'The rites of burial and sacrifice were sanctioned both by fear of the dead becoming vengeful demons and by the hope that the dead would become a benevolent god. Such a fear and such a hope underlie all of Chinese religion.'[6]

About 2,000 years ago Buddhism reached China with a new concept of the nature of self which merged with the popular ideas deriving from the remote past. One of the Buddha's fundamental teachings was the nonexistence of a 'soul' in any permanent sense. However, for the Chinese it seemed only rational that if one accepts the idea of *karma* there must be some continuing agent to carry out the process of *karma*. As popularly understood, *karma* became a sort of merit and demerit system determined by one's past actions. A person reaps in the next life what he has sown in the present. This concept not only provides an incentive to do good and to shun evil, but gives an explanation of why bad things sometimes happen to good people.

As Buddhism spread among the Chinese it became accommodated into the ancient ancestral beliefs and so the concept of the soul became an integral part of Chinese Buddhism. This resulted in a type of purgatory system based upon karmic principles. The Buddhist monks became responsible for the funeral and memorial rites.

There were therefore two inter-related paradigms of the nature of humanity among the Chinese. The first was based on yin and yang, and the other imported from Indian belief in *karma*.

Knowing

Tao by very definition is beyond knowing, and impossible to talk about. This very refusal to try and define Tao has overtones in that the ideas of Tao are not really ideas at all but ways in which one views reality. Thus Lao-tzu defines three stances that may be assumed after hearing about the Tao. First, a man of the highest ability will put it into practice; a man of middling ability will feel anxious about it; a man of little ability will laugh at it.

Figure 6.2 The Chinese symbol for yin and yang, the negative and positive elements of experience

The key symbol of Taoism is the circle of interpenetrating light and dark (see Figure 6.2). The symbol insinuates that reality emerges through the interaction of all the polarities that enter in our experience, and that reality cannot ever be defined except in terms of interactions and relatives. The mystical quality of this way of thinking is illustrated by the writings of Lao-tzu:

> Once Chuang Chou dreamt he was a butterfly, a butterfly flitting and fluttering about, happy with himself and doing as he pleased. He didn't know he was Chuang Chou. Suddenly he woke up and there he was, solid and unmistakable Chuang Chou. But he didn't know if he was Chuang Chou who had dreamt he was a butterfly, dreaming he was Chuang Chou.[7]

The philosophical Taoism is flourishing in the West today, but for the majority of Chinese it was too speculative. As with primal and folk societies worldwide, the concern of the ordinary people is merely to cope with the everyday issues of life.

How does one avoid disturbing the balance of yin and yang that can cause misfortune? Perhaps it is the long and tumultuous history of the Chinese that has made them a practical people seeking to cope with the changes that occur around them. They have sought to prepare themselves for these events by seeking to probe the secrets of their future fate by means of many methods of fortune telling. The art of divination goes back to prehistoric times, and this gradually evolved into the *I-Ching*, or *Book of Changes*. Almanacs are common in most Chinese homes and they contain a wide variety of information.[8]

Another common form of geomancy is *Fung shui*. Even today, in Hong Kong and Singapore, no modern building is constructed without consultation with a Fung shui expert to determine the best location. In Singapore, for example, a block of public housing flats had to be modified because the front doors faced each other – a bad Fung shui aspect – and people refused to live in them. The construction of the modern underground system in Hong Kong (Mass Transit Railway) was started with an invocation given by a multitude of Taoist priests. They paid respects to all the spirits of the earth who were about to have their domain violated.[9]

Consulting fortune sticks for the answers to problems is one of the most popular methods of divination amongst ordinary Chinese. The visitor who enters any temple in Hong Kong at virtually any time of the day is likely to find worshippers on their knees before the main altar, steadily shaking away at a bunch of bamboo sticks in a tubular container. The worshipper must ask a question clearly in his mind, and the answer will be given by the stick which jumps out of the container. The person will take this to the medium attached to the temple who will then interpret the Chinese character written on the particular stick.

To successfully cope with the seen and unseen world it is therefore necessary to have learning. This results in the Chinese respect for the scholar. However, this is not the same as in the West. In the West, the emphasis is more on the information one has, whilst in China it also includes the practical application which must be earned.[10]

Community

As with those societies holding to the primal worldview, the family is of great importance within the Chinese worldview. The Chinese say that 'to live at all is to live in relations', that is, relationship to other people.[11] Whilst Taoism primarily referred to 'other-worldly' matters, it was Confucianism which dealt with relationships of this world. Taoism and Confucianism complemented each other just as did the concepts of yin and yang.

Traditional Confucianism contains the notion of 'li' which is a process by which a person becomes more human as he enters into relations with others. The term *li* means ritual deportment in all social circumstances from the most weighty of religious ceremonies to the trivialities of daily etiquette.

Every individual is part of an almost endless chain of humanity of which the family is the central social unit. It is generally accepted that the most important human relationship was that between father and son called *xiao*, inadequately translated 'filial piety'. Xiao was a superior-inferior relationship meaning that a man's first duty was to his parents. As a Chinese proverb says, 'Under heaven, no parent is ever wrong.' The duty of the children, in theory at least, was to devote themselves to the welfare of their parents. It is for this reason that the Chinese are shocked at the way Westerners seem quite happy to place their aging parents in old people's homes.

The Confucian ethic has given every person a definite status in society and defines their relationship with others. There are distinctions between men and women, ruling authority and subjects, and between old and young. As a man gets older and his seniors die, so he gradually becomes more powerful in the family until he may become the head of the family. His importance is by virtue of his position, and not his own right as an individual.

Women are considered to be of a lower status than men. Their birth is attended by little of the rejoicing which surrounds that of a son. A daughter is considered a burden by the parents, and she has little opportunity for education and choice in her own marriage partner. Barrenness was one of the worst fears of the young bride, and her marriage was in a certain amount of danger until she had given birth to a son. It was not until old age that a woman would gain a measure of equality with a man, and this was gained through the family system and her having sons.

A person's status is linked with the concept of 'face'. This is a difficult term to describe in English. It is more than 'honour'. It is a valuable commodity which may be acquired and used. Loss of face is something which affects family first, but also the whole village. There is therefore a concept of collective shame.

The concept of ancestors is an important theme within the Chinese worldview, and this develops from the notion of the family extending from past generations onto the unborn in a similar way to that found in the primal worldview. The mutual dependency found within the living family extends backward in time to the ancestors. As Hsu writes:

> ... the departed ancestors continue, as in life, to assist their relatives in this world just as their living descendants can also lend a hand to them... The strength of this belief in a continuing 'social tie' is attested to by many popular tales.[12]

The central idea in the ancient Chinese religious rites was that 'all things originated from Heaven; people originated from their ancestors'.[13] By worshipping their ancestors, the Chinese harmonised the relations between the living and the dead. The supermarkets of Hong Kong sell wads of bank notes stamped 'HELL BANK' which are taken by the purchaser to be burned on the altar at the local temple. This money is believed to be transported to the unseen world for the use of an ancestor who may have need.

There are two great festivals for visiting family graves, the spring festival of Ching Ming and the autumn festival of Chung Yeung. Even in a modern business conscious city like Kowloon, many of the people leave their factories and journey to graves of their ancestors in the neighbouring hills. There the family will burn joss sticks and make offerings. They will then sit down happily beside, or even on Grandmother's grave to eat food and chat. Westerners often think that the Chinese lack respect for the departed, but that is to misunderstand the

Chinese concept of the dead. Dead does not mean departed, but no longer of this body. They are still part of the family.

Immortality has been a preoccupation with many Chinese resulting from the ancient Taoist beliefs. Some sages suggested the keeping of a certain diet or practising breathing exercises, but the main concern was to find a miracle drug which would transform the body in a moment. Some fantastic stories resulted, but no method was found. In practice, immortality is socially achieved through the lives of one's posterity. By depersonalising the ultimate reality the Chinese closed in upon themselves – the afterlife has become simply history immortalised.

Time

To the Chinese time has never been such an important factor as in the West. A rickshaw coolie would be paid for the distance covered, and not the length of time that it took him to cover the distance. Time is seen as stretching into the past and future, but it is not so much regarded as a valuable commodity as in the West. Punctuality is there the exception rather than the rule.

> 'The Chinese concept of time is more in the nature of an expansion of the present into both the past and the future with man occupying the centre of the stage. Rather than existing as an abstract quality, each "cycle" or period of time has definite limits which coincide with the beginning and end of a unified train of events. Furthermore, temporal relationships are practically indistinguishable from spacial relationships: an event (or an object) may be contiguous with or separated from another before it or after it, but there is not necessarily a causal relationship between them. In effect, time does not provide the Chinese with the same rational means of explanation and prediction which the American and Western concept yields in material cause and effect. The Chinese demonstrates a much greater situation-centredness and seeks an explanation for a specific happening in terms of other factors occurring at the same time as the event in question.... This view of time inclines the Chinese to integrate with the environment rather than master it and to adapt to a situation rather than change it.'[14]

Value

The Chinese view of man has no teaching of original sin, nor inherent depravity from which a person needs to be saved. Chinese philosophers never seemed to come to a conclusion as to whether man is good, bad or neutral. The majority view was that man was inherently good, but even those who would hold to the opposite view would only insist that man was inclined towards evil. Education was regarded as the means by which the unenlightened may be corrected and learn to behave as a gentleman.

The term *jen* is a collective name for the qualities which distinguish the polite classes from the vulgar. A gentleman was a man possessing the character of a gentleman, and not just one born of a noble family. It is important to realise that it was the concentration on character building which was the most important thing amongst the Chinese elite, and not the religious quest.

Confucius listed five qualities concerning 'jen': 'Politeness, liberality, good faith, diligence and generosity. Being polite, you will not be slighted; being liberal, you will win the people; having good faith, you will be trusted by others; having diligence, you will be successful; being generous, you will be worthy to employ others.'[15]

The most important element of such a character was right social relationships. Social harmony is of great importance. This was achieved when every person fulfils their appropriate duties of their station in life.

'Between father and son there is affection; between prince and minister there is integrity; between husband and wife there is a proper distance; between senior and junior there is proper precedence; between friend and friend there is faithfulness.'[16] Master Meng (*c* 390–305 BC)

The Chinese worldview compared

It has already been mentioned that the Chinese worldview has similarities to both the primal and Hindu worldview. However, there are some notable differences.

Both the Chinese and primal worldview perceive the cosmos as an integrated whole with an interpenetration of the visible and invisible, spiritual and material. The primal worldview sees a capriciousness within the spirit world whilst the Chinese have Tao which is conceived of as both Supreme Spirit and the inner law governing the universe. This gives to the Chinese worldview a stability and possibility for technological and social development.

Primal societies tend to be focused upon the tribe itself. Chinese society also tends to focus upon its own people and land. However, the social structure with its emphasis upon harmony, and everyone knowing their social place, allowed the growth of a complex and extensive society. This then allowed the development of a rich and complex civilisation. Whilst Primal societies showed a fragility in the face of world ideologies, the Chinese society was able to absorb new ideas within their existing worldview.

Both the Hindu and Chinese worldviews may be described as pantheistic. The Hindu form of pantheism regards 'reality' as being totally the 'Brahman' which (who) is beyond an illusory world. According the Chinese worldview one discovers the Tao which is not concealed in things, but actually revealed by them in the world. Thus, the Hindu worldview is world-denying in contrast to the Chinese which is world-affirming. The result is that the Chinese tend to have a very practical outlook upon the world. Most Chinese want little to do with gods and spirits only as far as they may keep them content.

Indian society venerates the saint whilst Chinese society respects the sage, and yet there is a marked difference between the two. Release in the Hindu worldview results from wisdom based upon an inner light. It is not a wisdom which can begin from the world so the individual is encouraged to look within. The Chinese worldview, on the other hand, perceives the scholar who is at once theoretical and practical. The Tao is a synthesis of the 'other world' and the 'this world'.

Buddhism was the only alien tradition to greatly modify Chinese culture, and it achieved this only by being itself greatly reinterpreted. Buddhism provided an answer for salvation not addressed by either Taoism or Confucianism. Salvation was presented on two levels. First, for a man capable of high understanding and discipline, salvation came through the enlightenment concerning the illusory nature of the world, and thus the release from the torments of human passions. However, there was a second way more suited to the ordinary person unable to achieve the philosophy of the Buddha. Buddha Sakyamuni was assisted by countless buddhas and bodhisattvas who helped those who longed for salvation. The bodhisattva was a person who had attained enlightenment and limitless powers that enabled him to become Buddha-like. However, he denied personal salvation so that he may devote his religious powers to helping others along the way. In popular thinking these buddhas and bodhisattvas became individualised deities.

The Communist takeover of China has undoubtedly caused many changes in thought and practice. Marxism with its secular worldview contrasts markedly with the traditional Chinese worldview. History has yet to show whether the ordinary Chinese peasant will convert to this secular philosophy, or whether they will interpret Marxist ideas within the ancient Chinese worldview. Hesselgrave has alluded to some of the parallels which already exist and could develop further in the future. They may 'replace the Tao with dialectic materialism; transmute the Yin and the Yang into thesis and antithesis; and continue to affirm man and the world'.[17]

Recent changes throughout the Communist world may eventually allow such a freedom amongst the Chinese people that the traditional worldview will once again be seen. When I was once talking to a Chinese friend in Canton about the cultural revolution under Mao, he quietly drew a long line on a piece of paper. Near the end of the line he drew a little blip. 'That,' he said, 'was the cultural revolution'.

Notes

1. Hesselgrave, David J. *Communicating Christ Cross-Culturally* (Zondervan Publishing House: Grand Rapids, 1978) p 175.
2. Bloomfield, Frena. *The Book of Chinese Beliefs* (Arrow Books: London, 1983) p 16.
3. Burkhardt, V.R. *Chinese Creeds and Customs* (South China Morning Post: Hong Kong, 1982) p 153.
4. Soo, Chee. *The Taoist Ways of Healing* (Aquarian Press: Wellingborough, 1986) pp 30–31.
5. Clayre, Alasdair. *The Heart of the Dragon* (Collins/Harvill: London, 1984) p 204.
6. Thompson, Laurence G. *Chinese Religion* (Wadsworth Pub. Co.: Belmont, 1989) p 12.
7. *The Complete Works of Chuang-Tzu* (Columbia University Press: New York, 1968) p 49.
8. Bloomfield, *op cit*, pp 146–157.
9. Bloomfield, *ibid*, p 25.
10. Yutang, Lin. *My Country and my people* (Heinemann: London, 1962) p 73.
11. Porras, Nancy. 'The Chinese View of Self', *International Journal of Frontier Missions*, October 1985, pp 305–314.
12. Hsu, Francis L.K. *Americans and Chinese* (The University Press of Hawaii: Hawaii, 1953) p 252.
13. Yunan-Kwei, Wei. 'Historical Analysis of Ancestor Worship in Ancient China', *Christian Alternatives to Ancestor Practices* by Bong Rin Ro (Asian Theological Association, 1985) p 123.
14. Stewart, Edward C. *American Cultural Patterns: A Cross-Cultural Perspective* (Society for Intercultural Education: La Grange Park, 1972) p 67.
15. Waley, Arthur. *Analects of Confucius* (Allen & Unwin: London, 1938) XVII, 6.
16. Thompson, p 14 *op cit*.
17. Hesselgrave, *op cit*, p 179.

7

MUHAMMAD AND THE MESSAGE:
The Islamic Worldview

The last great world religion to develop was Islam. It burst out of Arabia in the seventh century and transformed the map of the medieval world. It came with one over-riding message which provides the key to the Islamic worldview – there is only one God.

> He is Allah, than whom there is no other God, the Sovereign Lord, the Holy One, Peace, the Keeper of the Faith, the Guardian, the Majestic, the Compeller, the Superb.[1] (*Sura* 59:23)

Muhammad ibn 'Abdulla of the Banu Hashim of Quraish was born in Mecca in about AD 570. At that time the Arabs were divided into many tribal confederacies, and followed a primal religion believing in many gods and spirits. Muhammad reacted against these polytheistic beliefs, and withdrew for periods of religious meditation. During one of these periods, he claimed that visions came to him through the angel Gabriel. At first he was uncertain of the validity of these revelations, but gained confidence as his wife Khadija reassured him. Although he gained a following, he was opposed by many of his country-men, and had to flee to Medina. Against all odds Muhammad continued to persevere and finally achieved victory with all the Arab tribes converting to monotheism.

Muslims argue strongly for a sharp distinction between Islam and the traditional beliefs of the Arab people in the period known as the *Jahiliya* (ignorance). The name 'Allah' is a simple contraction of 'Al Ilah' – the God. The Qur'an itself (Sura 39:4) provides evidence that the name was used by traditional religionists to describe the supreme deity. Many of the traditional worldview themes were transformed and given an entirely new content within the developing Islamic worldview. Many key Islamic terms reflect a desert environment. One therefore sees similarity and yet marked differences between the primal and Islamic worldviews.

The conversion to monotheism revitalised the Arab people with a religious zeal which produced an astounding military expansion that established a mighty Arab Empire. Islam was quickly transformed from being merely a tribal religion to become a world religion spreading from West Africa to Indonesia in the East. The unifying force were the revelations of Muhammad written down after his death as the Qur'an. The text was written in Arabic which became the language of the Islamic civilisations, and also the langauge of this dominant worldview.

Muhammad was certainly influenced by the ideas of both Judaism and Christianity, the two other major monotheistic religions. One can see many similarities with regards to the worldview themes, but there are also some striking differences. It is however because of the similarities that the followers of these religions have been able to understand each other's views, and therefore recognise where they differ. An awareness of the differences is one of the reasons why there has been such a history of tension between the great monotheistic religions.

Like the previous worldviews considered, the Islamic worldview is broad and diverse in nature. We will therefore concentrate upon those themes particularly characteristic of the Arab world. Malise Ruthven prefers to speak about 'the Qur'anic Worldview' because Arabic is so important to the culture, and the Qur'an is the key to Arabic.[2] We will here speak of Islamic worldview themes.

Islamic worldview themes

The Cosmos

Islam begins and ends with the concept that there is no God but Allah. Allah is all-powerful, sovereign and unknowable. The fact of the oneness of God is the dominant theme within Islamic theology where it is known as 'Tawhid', but its influence spreads throughout Muslim culture. The fact of one God means that those who are submitted to him are one people practising a oneness in their worship. The 'Hajj' is an expression of this oneness when Muslims come together from all nations and classes dressed in a common simple garb to be involved in a common practice of worship. Tawhid is seen in the common direction for prayer which is towards Mecca, the birth place of the prophet. Tawhid is also seen in the fast of Ramadan which occurs during the same month for Muslims throughout the world.

Islam draws a clear distinction between the Creator God, Allah, and his creation. This distinction between Creator and creation is the key characteristic of any theistic worldview, and is found in Judaism and Christianity. In Islam the domain over which the Creator presides is divided into the 'unseen' (*al ghaib*) and 'seen' (*al shahada*). Only the latter is accessible to man, though he has knowledge of the existence of the former, derived from revelation.

Not only is the 'seen' world populated, but so is the 'unseen'. Although Islam is opposed to a plurality of gods, as found in primal religions, it is not opposed to a plurality of spirits. The unseen is considered to be populated by two forms of spiritual beings: angels, who carry out the commands of Allah, and *jinn*, who cause harm under the leadership of Satan. The antithesis between good and evil spirits is another distinction between the Islamic and primal worldviews.

Whether good or evil, all beings are subject to Allah, and in the final analysis do his bidding. The universe is ultimately under the control of its Creator. Allah is all-powerful! No wonder this leads to a sense of fatalism amongst Muslims. God's will must be done! If a person dies, or suffers misfortune, it is the will of Allah. Likewise if a person has success it is also the will of Allah.

The Self

Islam sees mankind as the creatures of Allah and subject to his will. They exist in dependence upon God and are sustained by his power with the purpose of expressing adoration to their Creator. Human beings are totally subject to the will of Allah, and so must submit to his will. The very word 'muslim' means one who is submitted to God.

All human beings stand towards God in the relation of a slave towards his master. Slaves have no rights. He has no intrinsic value, but to do what his master commands. He is to obey, and in obeying he finds his worth. To the individual who accepts and fulfils these demands in full, God, in his mercy, may grant certain privileges.

In response to the fear of God, people must submit to the will of God, humbling themselves, and undertaking the duties and responsibilities of Muslims. These human responsibilities are essentially contained in the 'Five Pillars' of Islam:

1 Confession of Faith by repetition of the Word of Witness (*shahada*).
2 Regular performance of ritual prayers at the appointed five times each day (*salat*).
3 The giving of alms (*zakat*).
4 Observance of the annual fast in the month of Ramadan.
5 Pilgrimage to Mecca (*hajj*).

Over and above these five duties there are certain other obligations given by Allah for right conduct now formulated in the Shariah law which will be returned to later.

There is an inconsistency within Islam which is not easily answered. How can God be on one hand completely sovereign and yet on the other hand require humans to forsake their idols and mend their ways? This paradox cannot be reconciled intellectually, and remains in an uneasy synthesis within Islam. There are limits to human knowledge, just as there are limits to human behaviour. Perhaps it is illustrated by an Arab proverb: 'Trust in Allah – but tether your camel first.'

Success and failure, sickness and health come from the sovereign will of Allah. Death is not the end. Some whom Allah has chosen will enjoy a heaven filled with sensual delights, of which the present existence is a foretaste. Others will know the punishment of hell. The fortunes of humans will be allotted at the Day of Judgement.

Knowing

In Islam, it is the revelation which was given by Allah which is all important, not intellectual knowledge achieved by analysis, as with the secular worldview, or the wisdom of enlightenment, as in the Hindu worldview. It is the Qur'an which is the embodiment of that revelation and so for the Muslim becomes beyond question or reason. The Qur'an is holy and powerful. The importance is not in understanding it, but the significance depends on its own intrinsic power. Thus, the Qur'an should be memorised, not necessarily understood. Learning is therefore by rote and not primarily by deductive logic.

There is a major difference between the understanding of revelation in Islam and in Christianity. In Islam, the inspiration came directly to Muhammad, and was transmitted orally and eventually written down in the Qur'an word-for-word, in a manner similar to dictation. In fact, Muslims often say that the Qur'an has been written from eternity, on tablets of gold, by the throne of Allah. For this reason the Qur'an is regarded as possessing a quality of spiritual power. Within folk Islam, a verse from the Qur'an is spoken to protect one from a *jinn*, or a few verses may be written on a parchment and worn as a charm for protection from curses.

Christianity, on the other hand, has considered that the Bible as the revelation of God has been expressed through human writers. It has reflected the personality of the individual, and yet it has not lost the purity and accuracy of the divine revelation. As J.I. Packer has written, 'God completely adapted his inspiring activity to the cast of mind, outlook, temperament, interests, literary habits and stylistic idiosyncrasies of each writer.'[3] The revelation thus became incarnated within human culture rather than being distinct from it as in Islamic thought.

Another contrast concerns the nature of the revelation. In Christianity the revelation is primarily of the character of God. Islam, on the other hand, does not reveal the nature of God who is considered unknowable, but his laws. Islam is therefore a religion of law which mankind should obey without question.

Community

Community is an important aspect of Muslim cultures. The faithful individuals who gathered around Muhammad formed not only a religious community, but also a political one. No distinction was drawn between the religious and the political aspects of community. For this reason, Islam can only be fully realised within the context of an Islamic state. This populace is the 'ummah', the community of believers.

An individual therefore has two principal sources of social identity – his family and his religious community. An individual's first allegiance is to his family, that is the extended family rather than the nuclear family found in Western society. The Muslim family is a unity which cares for each member of the family, and old people are regarded as those to be honoured.

Within Islamic society there is a marked distinction between male and female roles which affects all areas of social life. A man takes a dominant role with regards to his wife. She is often called his 'garden' into which he may go and have pleasure and produce children. A man takes the public roles within the family, whilst the wife remains in the seclusion of the home. The man is concerned with business and social decisions, whilst the wife looks after the babies, cooks the food, and manages the home.

The second social area is that of the Muslim community as a whole. At times the religious demands of the community can over-ride even those of family obligations. The basic social institutions of the Muslim community are laid down in detail in the Qur'an, together with other definite rulings relating to daily life. The community is regulated by a system of regulations known as the Shariah (law) which draws strongly upon the sayings concerning the Prophet in the 'Summas'.

Time

Time is regarded as a linear series of events and not as a linear dimension of some precious commodity as in the secular worldview. Time is not considered an item of value which can be accumulated or budgeted. Efficiency is therefore not of prime importance as in Western society as many Westerners have found to their frustration.

Personal relationships are more important than time. 'In the United States a salesman may walk away from the first meeting with an order in his pocket. But in the Arab world, several meetings of social visiting may be required before one can get down to business.'4 Bargaining is another example of this aspect of Islamic culture. The act of trading is not considered to be merely some mechanism for economic transaction, but it is an opportunity of social interaction which allows the buyer and seller the opportunity of knowing each other's strengths and weaknesses.

The immutable nature of the Qur'an means that change in general is considered to be something to be resisted. The Qur'an cannot be up-dated or rewritten. Thus, the prevalent time-orientation points back to the golden age of Islam, rather than to the future as with the secular worldview.

Value

Ethical considerations are based solely upon the sovereignty of God who will judge all human beings on the last day. In addition to the 'Five Pillars' mentioned earlier, human beings must follow the Shariah law which is regarded as 'the revelation of

God to man, to order his affairs, guide his life and give him an answer for every question of right and wrong'.[5] It includes directions on such subjects as marriage, foods, and usury. Much of the law is based upon how Muhammad and the early Muslims acted and felt in everyday situations. Islam therefore presents a recognised pattern of outward behaviour which is universal in its application to every society.

The heart of Shariah law is the family, and this is reflected in that good behaviour is related to the family. The honour of a person derives from his family. Honour is perceived almost as a commodity which may be passed from one generation to another. All good achievements build up a man's honour. Honour finds expression in maintaining a proper relationship between the sexes. A man of honour sees to it that his daughters or sisters do not act sensually towards men. Sexual crimes are considered crimes relating to a man's honour. If a person brings shame on another it must be revenged, and frequently this leads to bloodshed and vendettas.

Hospitality is another important value in any Arab family, and is closely linked to the notion of honour. By practising hospitality lavishly, one enhances one's reputation. If a visitor is not received hospitably, the failure reflects on the honour of the entire tribe or family and blemishes its reputation. Much of what has been seen as Arab nationalism in recent years reflects this particular theme. Israel can have no peace as long as the honour of the Arabs has been offended.

It can be seen that the Islamic worldview is one in which an external, immutable law has been given to mankind. This law touches every part of life, and yet it fails to meet the inner needs of the human heart. The revelation from Allah has been given in its totality, and has been sealed as the Qur'an. The door to contemporary experience of the numinous appears to have been closed. Perhaps this is the reason that Sufism, the mystical dimension of Islam, came into being.

Mystical Islam

It has been estimated that between one-third and one-half of the Muslim world is involved in some form of Sufi brotherhood.[6] Sufism has a long and often turbulent history within the main fold of Islam. The survival and growth of Sufism reveals the inherent weakness within the orthodox Islamic worldview to meet an inner need. The Shariah does not legislate for the conscience, but confines itself to gathering the faithful around the rites and observances of the Islamic community without troubling the inner life. Sufism addresses that missing dimension.

Sufis claim that it is possible to enter into a living experience with the divine through the mystic experience. This, they claim, is the deeper truth which lies behind the external observances of the Shariah. As with all mystics, the Sufi places great value upon the mystic knowledge which comes not by education, but by experience. It is a knowledge which cannot be taught, but can be shared with one who has had a similar encounter.

Mystics of all monotheistic religions in their very experience with divinity tend towards a pantheism. 'The whole of Sufism rests on the belief that when the individual self is lost, the Universal Self is found, or, in religious language, that ecstasy affords the only means by which the soul can directly communicate and become united with God.'[7]

The poetry of the great Sufi Jalal al-Din Rumi (d. AD 1273) illustrates this quest. He uses the imagery of the reed-pipe to portray the mystic's desolate cry to God.

> Harken to this Reed forlorn,
> Breathing, ever since 'twas torn
> From its rushy bed, a strain
> Of impassioned love and pain.
>
> The secret of my song, though near,
> None can see and none can hear.
> Oh, for a friend to know the sign
> And mingle all his soul with mine!

'Tis the flame of Love that fired me,
'Tis the wine of Love inspired me.
Would'st thou learn how lovers bleed,
Harken, harken to the Reed![8]

In a desire for the mystic quest there grew in Islam systems both for traversing the path (*tariq*), and Sufi orders (*Ta'ifas*). The techniques to gain the mystic experiences have been many. Chanting and breathing control have been commonly used in Central Asia. The name 'Allah' is chanted with vigour until the tongue and lips can say it no more, and there exists nothing but the impression of the word in the depths of the heart. Within the Ottoman Empire, the whirling dance of the Dervish provided a means of drawing the devotee into a union with the divine. From India, the Sufi made use of yogi practices to help him in his quest. Music, rhythms, drumming and even drugs have been used by the seeker.

The organisation of Sufis into orders brought about a standardisation within the order, and a growing political influence which helped the spread of Islam. Usually the founders of such orders were possessors of a particular type of charisma known as 'baraka'. When these men died a tomb was built over the site, and this became a place of pilgrimage. It is believed that even to touch the tomb will transfer baraka which will cause healing and blessing.

The future of Islam

The expansion of Islam was due to the revitalisation of Arab society through what is relatively a simple message. First, the message spoke of there being only one God, the creator of all. Secondly, mankind must submit to the will of God as revealed by the prophet Muhammad. This relatively simple message presented by a fast developing civilisation resulted in the conversion of many primal societies. What does the future hold for Islam? To surmise what may happen we can only look at the trends which are already evident.

Contact with Christianity

As with most monotheistic religions, Islam and Christianity share many common themes with regards to their worldview. It is because they show such marked similarity that the two religious systems have clashed. Both are missionary religions seeking to present a similar message of one creator God. Both claim to have the revelation of God presented in a holy book. Both have produced important empires which have expanded politically and economically.

The Crusades provide an important historical illustration of this clash. A study of the history of the Crusades shows that the truth is far removed from the idealised stories of Sir Walter Scott, and the image of 'Good King Richard'. The Crusades revealed the worst and best of Christian Europe and the Muslim Middle East.[9] The main reasons for the Crusades were mainly commercial where the Venetian states wanted to gain the monopoly of the trade links with the Arab world which had been dominated by the Byzantine Empire.

Western Imperialism finally began to make an impression in the Middle East when Napoleon conquered Egypt. Within a century, most of the Muslim world was under the domination of the Christian nations of Europe. This was only to produce additional hatred and resentment from the Muslim peoples – it was an offence to their honour, and a reproach to their religion. The establishment of the state of Israel in 1948, and its continual support by Christian nations, remains as a continual shame to the Muslim world.

During the last two centuries there has been renewed Christian missionary work amongst Muslims. The impact upon the Muslim world has been little, partly through cultural insensitivity, and partly through association with the European colonial powers. However, in more recent years there has been a growing awareness amongst Christians of the need to understand and appreciate the Muslim culture and explore the riches of this worldview.[10]

Although there are many similarities in worldview between the monotheistic religions, there are also some important differences. The difference in the concept of the nature of God has some major repercussions as regards to an understanding of love, community, and salvation. Likewise, the nature of sin is markedly different, and is not merely concerned with the actions of man, as in Islam, but the inward thoughts as well. Finally, there is the understanding of the nature of revelation which contrasts markedly with that understood in the West.

Secularisation

It is perhaps with the single fact of the discovery of oil in the Middle East that one has seen a change in the attitude of Muslim peoples. Oil has given to the Muslim world an economic and political power for use against the dominant Christian world. The oil is believed by Muslims to have been placed there by Allah, and is given for the propagation of Islam. For this reason, Saudi Arabia and other Muslim countries are using their new found wealth for the extension of Islam. These countries are using their oil money to build new prestigious mosques in major cities throughout the world. They are establishing major radio and television stations. They are making large quantities of literature available to propagate Islam. Islam has suddenly taken on an offensive which has shaken many in the West.

It has already been mentioned that the time orientation of Islam is essentially resistant to change. The newly acquired oil money has given the Muslim nations the invitation to change, and introduce the new technology of the West. This has placed many Muslim nations in a dilemma. How much does one accept of the Western culture along with its material technology? Some nations have sought to do a careful balancing act between accepting the comforts of the new technology, and in so doing allowing the influence of the so-called immorality of the West. Other nations have reacted away from the decadence of the West into the 'Islamic Revolution'.

The Revolutionary Alternative

The dramatic changes within Iran have left many Western observers amazed. Here was a nation which seemed to be one of the most progressive in Western terms suddenly changing and reverting to a traditional Muslim society. This whole process reveals the growing tension which was occurring between the worldview of traditional Islam and the secular worldview from the West. The tension had to be resolved, either by the conversion to Western culture, or a reaction from it. The honour of the Muslims would not allow them to accept the culture of their former rulers. No wonder there had to be a backlash against Western culture which lead to the cries, 'Death to America! Death to Russia! Death to Britain!'

Adapting to the world society

In general, it seems as though Islam will neither wither away under the influence of secularism nor totally return to the traditional ways of the past. It seems mostly to be struggling to adapt itself, and to co-exist with its contemporary environment.

This struggle is seen amongst the Muslim communities in Britain. Their religion has kept them as distinct social entities, and yet their children face the tensions of living between two very different worldviews. On the one hand, the mosque provides the focus for their sense of community, and the Qur'anic schools as a means of training the young generation in the traditional ways. On the other hand, their schools present a secular science, and a freedom from social restraint.

The Sufi Way

The growing interest amongst the secular West in mystic phenomena has caused a growth of interest in Sufism. How far this form of mysticism will spread, within a world of many competing philosophies, is unclear.

The Islamic worldview is one which is still strong and vital. It continues to claim the allegiance of millions within the world today and will continue to influence a large proportion of the population of the world in the coming years.

Notes

1. Pickthall, Mohammed. *The Meaning of the Glorious Koran* (Mentor Books: London) p 394.
2. Ruthven, Malise. *Islam in the World* (Penguin Books Ltd: Harmondsworth, 1984) p 101.
3. Packer, J.I. *Fundamentalism and the Word of God* (IVP: Leicester, 1963) p 79.
4. Matheny, Tim. *Reaching the Arabs: a felt need approach* (William Carey Library: Pasadena, 1981) p 31.
5. Cooper, Anne. *Ishmael my Brother* (MARC: Bromley, 1985) p 111.
6. Cooper, ibid. p 103.
7. Nicholson, Reynold. *The Mystics of Islam* (Routledge and Kegan Paul: London, 1963) p 59.
8. Arberry, A.J. *Sufism: An account of the mystics of Islam* (Unwin Paperbacks: London, 1979) p 111.
9. Maalouf, Amin. *The Crusades through Arab Eyes* (Al Saqi Books: London, 1984).
10. Parshall, Phil. *New Paths in Muslim Evangelism* (Baker Book House: Grand Rapids, 1980).

PART III

Worlds in Change

8

WORLDVIEW CHANGE

Heraclitus, a Greek philosopher of the sixth century BC, noted, in going to his favourite bathing spot at the river, that people never put their feet twice in the same water. Change, he concluded, is a continual factor in every person's experience.

Cultures are ever changing. Cultures may be likened to the flow of a river. Sometimes the river flows fast as it hurtles down steep gorges pushing all before it. The river may cascade over cliffs as it changes direction forming dramatic waterfalls. At other times the river meanders slowly across flat plains leisurely changing direction as it continues on towards lower ground. Some rivers merge with others as they continue their endless pursuit towards the sea.

Throughout history peoples have migrated across the surface of the globe, traders have spread the latest products of technological invention, and exponents of new religions have taken their beliefs to those who have not previously heard. In the past four hundred years the whole process has gathered momentum, and continues to do so. The main cause for this has been the spread of the European peoples across the face of the world. The Europeans have taken with them their language, technology and culture. This has caused radical changes for some societies, and influenced all others.

The development of ships, cars, trains, and planes have made transport easier and swifter. People who once would never have met now come into contact. Radio and television allow news and ideas to be conveyed around the world in a matter of seconds. The world has indeed become a 'global village'.

These new means of communication have brought an exchange of trade goods and Western technology, but most of all, new ideas. Not even the political and social barriers of East and West, and North and South have prevented the flow of these ideas. Assumptions which were once held above contradiction are now being questioned. Traditional worldview themes are in the process of change.

At first the flow was mainly from West to East. It was the Europeans who took their civilisation to the indigenous peoples of Africa, Asia and America. But, channels of communication work in both directions. During the last one hundred years the flow has also begun to occur from East to West. People from the East have settled in Europe bringing with them their own way of life and beliefs. Hindu, Buddhist, and Islamic ideas have thus penetrated into European cultures.

Social change

Sociologists have distinguished two main processes by which a culture changes: innovation and diffusion. An innovation is that which has been generated from within the society. It may be anything from new religious beliefs to technological discovery, but the essential factor is that it has been initiated by a member of that society. In most cases these are minor and almost imperceptible changes, but they may be radical ideas which cause major changes within that society.

Within all societies there are those individuals who tend to question the accepted assumptions and come up with new ideas. They may be regarded on the one hand as radicals, revolutionaries, and disturbers of the peace, or on the other hand, they are accepted as scientists, explorers, and scholars. These innovators question the accepted assumptions concerning the nature of the world, and in so doing provide new answers.

People are constantly changing what they do and how they do it. In the telling of a story an individual may delete some parts whilst elaborating others. A person may wear their clothes in a different way, or build their house with different materials. Some innovations are adopted by others and become part of the collective behaviour of the society, whilst others are quickly forgotten.

One illustration of the change of worldview themes has been one which has occurred within Western society. At the end of the seventeenth century, the belief in God was universally held in Europe. Scholars and theologians would debate the finer points of their assumptions, but all would ascribe to the same basic set of worldview themes. The main assumption being that there is an absolute Being and so there is absolute truth. As Francis Schaeffer has shown, absolutes imply antithesis, so that one can accept the formula, 'If you have A it is not non-A'.[1]

It was the German philosopher Hegel (1770-1831) who first questioned this assumption. He proposed that, instead of thesis and antithesis, one has thesis and antithesis resulting in a synthesis. What this seemingly abstract, theoretical discussion did was to question one of the fundamental assumptions of the Western worldview. In rejecting the theme that there is an absolute it led to the conclusion that there are no moral absolutes – all is relative. Other philosophers were later to take up this notion, and develop the ideas in the areas of art, literature, and science. New scientific theories developed based upon the concept of evolution. If there is no absolute creator then there must be some other cause for the world coming into being.

The final result was that Western society moved gradually from being essentially theistic in its worldview to being secular. What is more interesting is that the majority of the population did not even appreciate the nature of the movement. They simply drifted with the current of new ideas and formulation. The success of technology and science seemed to provide proof of the effectiveness of the ideas which were being propounded. Technology made life more comfortable, and so the population gradually accepted the worldview themes of secularism.

The church has often been slow to appreciate the nature of the changes which have occurred. Some theologians have accepted the secularised worldview and have sought to redraft theology in terms of these new worldview themes. They have regarded this as being 'modern' and 'scientific'. This was widely publicised as 'God-is-dead Theology'.

Diffusion is a second way in which new elements are introduced into a society. Diffusion consists of 'borrowing' or adopting elements from another society. This process is very common, and Ralph Linton says that less than 10% of the elements within any culture can be attributed to each society's own intentions.[2] The spread of the manufacture of paper is a good example of diffusion by means of direct contact. The invention of paper is attributed to the Chinese Ts'ai Lun in AD 105. Within fifty years paper was being made in many places in central China. By the year AD 264, it is found in Chinese Turkestan, and from there it progressed Westwards. By AD 751 it had reached Samarkand; AD 793 Baghdad; AD 900 Egypt; AD 1100 Morocco; AD 1189 France; 1391 Germany; 1494 England. Generally the pattern of accepting the borrowed invention was the same in each case. Paper was first imported into the area as luxury goods, then in ever increasing quantities. Finally, the local manufacture of paper was begun.

There is a temptation to view the process of diffusion as being similar to throwing a stone into a pond, and seeing the concentric ripples spread over the water. This is an oversimplification of the way diffusion occurs. Not all cultural elements are borrowed as readily as paper manufacture.

Diffusion is, firstly, a selective process in which some elements are accepted and others not. One example of selective diffusion is seen with the Japanese who have borrowed many items from Chinese culture, but have rejected others. Although foot binding was accepted by the Chinese, it was regarded as repugnant to the Japanese.

Secondly, some items diffuse more readily than others, usually because its value is easily observed such as with the use of paper. Mechanical processes or physical activities are easy to demonstrate, and so are accepted or rejected on their merits. Concepts and ideas, on the other hand, are more difficult to communicate effectively. Coca-Cola has become accepted worldwide, but not the Christian concept of the Trinity.

Thirdly, in many cases the element is accepted, but it is adapted to the needs of the particular culture and harmonised with the culture as a whole. This is the process of syncretism. This form of process occurs most readily when the diffusing element is complex and abstract such as with a religion. The ideas are only partially understood, and the people interpret them in terms of their existing worldview.

The process of diffusion is often encouraged by a person who advocates the particular change. Salesmen are a primary example from Western culture. Their aim is to show the value of their particular product and encourage its purchase.

Writers such as Wallace,[3] and Tippett[4] have tried to look at the nature of how worldviews change following contact with other cultures. The growing interaction between societies results in increased social stress. Tippett speaking particularly of primal societies describes four basic patterns of change which may occur within a society as a result of this stress.[5] We will now turn to consider these four common patterns which are demoralisation, submersion (here called syncretism), conversion and revitalisation (see Figure 8.1).

Demoralisation

As mentioned in the discussion of the primal worldview, it has been primal societies which have known the shattering impact of dominant cultures. Many once productive communities have disappeared altogether. Others survive only as tiny groups, with too few people to provide the numbers and balance required to maintain their traditions and culture.

One example is the fate of the indigenous people of Tasmania. Between 1803, the year of initial British settlement, and 1869, the entire indigenous population of Tasmania was wiped out. The settlers hunted the blacks for sport, shooting the men in cold blood and raping the women. In 1869 Truganina, the last member of a once gentle people, died at the age of seventy.[6]

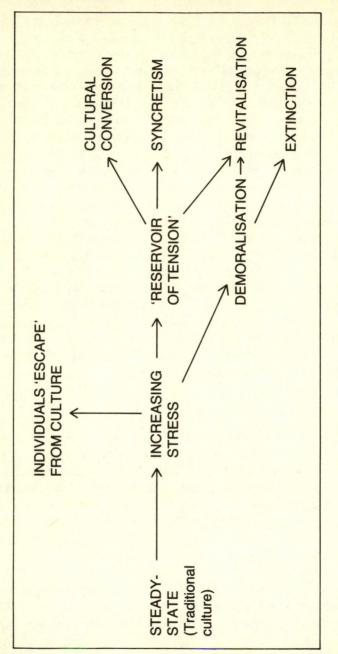

Figure 8.1 Patterns of culture change

Another such tribe are the Nambiquara of the Amazon forest.[7] Their first contact with the European was in 1911, at which time they were a stone-age people numbering about 20,000. In the 1930s a few settlers began to move into the area, and Roman Catholic priests began to work amongst them. After the second world war, rubber tappers moved into the forest area, and started to use the Nambiquara as conscript labour. Good money was paid for the work, but the cost of food was inflated so that the workers were always in debt to the 'Rubber King'.

Along with the white man came the white man's illnesses, and especially influenza and measles. No one seems to know which of these illnesses was to cause the death of so many of the Nambiquara, but in 1945 nineteen out of every twenty of the population died. This 95% reduction in the population had a devastating effect upon the society. Families were torn apart, children orphaned, wives were widowed. One village now contains the survivors of forty-three villages. The world had come to an end! Women no longer wanted to have children because they saw no point in them being born into a world they saw as falling apart. They were a depressed people, a weakened people, a people who needed time to recover. But time is not a thing that they had because the white settlers continued to press into their land. They are now settled into a reservation some 200 miles long by 50 miles wide. The soil is very acid and little grows.

It was not until 1960 that a serious attempt was made to learn their language. Theirs is a difficult language with tones, glottal stops, and long words. The Nambiquara know that they cannot cope with Brazilian culture, and they are easily pushed around by outsiders. They have not as yet found a way of resisting the outside pressure. Another tribe in close proximity has learnt the Portuguese language, and has started making artifacts for trade.

The Nambiquara are a dispirited people who attribute the epidemic to white man's black magic. They try to make sense of what has happened to them as a people in terms of their old worldview, but these traditions have obviously failed. They need a new worldview which will enable them to cope with the new and changing world in which they find themselves. It is not acceptable to leave them isolated in their scrub land, as some writers have suggested of such tribal people. They are part of the family of man and should not be locked up into a human zoo. By the very nature of the increasing population of the world they will not be left in isolation too long. People with a stronger spirit will eventually invade their remaining land. The Nambiquara need a new worldview and with it will come a new hope. They are like a person who has been bereaved. They need a new focus for their life. Often missionaries are criticised as being the fore-runners of Western civilisation which destroys such people, but what is often forgotten is that Western civilisation is pressing into these communities irrespective of missionary work. Oil and mineral prospectors, farmers looking for new land, industry cutting down the tropical forests are all pointing to the demise of primal societies. These advocates of Western civilisation come with no message of hope for the isolated peoples of the world. Surely here is a case where the coming of the Christian gospel is needed.

Conversion

By the term conversion, what is meant is not so much religious conversion, but cultural conversion. An alternative term which may be used is 'acculturation' which may be defined as the learning of a new culture. Politically it has often been called 'assimilation'. This was a policy employed in the United States at the end of the last century when the native Indians were herded onto reservations and taught the white man's ways.

> Most of the Indian children in the Northwest Territories boarded at the schools where they were being educated. In 1893 Mr Hayter Reed, superintendent of Indian Affairs, made their purpose clear: 'In the boarding or industrial schools the pupils are removed for a long time from the leadings of this uncivilised life and receive constant care and attention.' By removing the children from their

parents, dressing them in the clothes common to the southern whites and banning the use of native languages and native religious observances, whites hoped that these children would reject their traditional worldview and way of life and be converted to white civilisation.[8]

The process of conversion can also occur in more subtle ways. In some cases one can see individuals leave their village for the apparent excitement of the city. There they find some menial job which provides them with food and shelter, and maybe they will find a woman to live with them. In the new situation, they can try some of the culture of the city – drink, immorality, theft. When they return to their home village they are regarded with a new respect as they have new prized items such as a watch, cloth, white man's clothes, or even a transistor radio. Yet, more than that they have an inner restlessness born out of the limitations of the village, and the failure of the traditional ideas to answer the new questions which have come to his mind. Soon they return to the city.

Cultural conversion also occurs through education and especially schools. Throughout Africa and Asia, parents and children have been quick to see that one of the most effective paths to the wealth of the West is that of Western education. Parents get themselves into debt in order for their children to attend school, and to pass the next set of examinations. Only a few of the most lucky actually reach the prized positions of scholarships at a university. However, these few are enough to encourage a thousand hopefuls to work for the prized position. What neither the parent or student realises is that schools not only provide the prized white man's learning, but it changes the basic assumptions of the young scholar. He, or she, wants to be like his teacher, not like his unschooled father.

If the young people have been educated out of their traditional cultures, and they cannot achieve the educational qualifications to advance to university, where do they turn? They often drift to the city. There they turn to crime and prostitution. This has been stimulated by another force for cultural conversion, tourism. As the Western peoples have become more wealthy they have travelled first to the beauty spots of their own countries, then to those of neighbouring nations, but now it is almost to the ends of the earth.

In 1988, the first British conference on the social anthropology of tourism was organised.[9] Numerous papers were presented concerning sex-tourism. Thailand, Malaysia, and Philippines are well-known centres of this business. In the Caribbean one finds the 'beach bums' who trade on the stereotype of black males' sexual prowess. In Gambia, tourism has resulted in 1,500 young Gambian males being befriended by wealthy, older Swedish ladies who have taken them home as their 'toy-boys'.

Tourism, Western education, mass-media, and the process of urbanisation have all been major influences upon the many societies of planet earth. World organisations such as the United Nations have established a network of Nation States with interlinking bureaucratic structures. However, we must not be deluded into thinking that all people are rushing to merge into the common world culture.

When a society is strong and proud of its culture, it is not as easy for an individual to convert to another culture. The sense of group identity tends to weld the community together as a coherent whole. A person who leaves the community in which he was reared is often branded as a traitor and excluded from the community. This is most clearly seen when a Muslim becomes a Christian. He may then have to face the penalty of being rejected by the 'Ummah' (community), his wife may be taken from him, or he may have to pay the ultimate penalty of death.

The transition from one allegiance to another is easiest when the whole community adopts the new beliefs. This is what has been called a 'people movement' by Donald McGravan in his study of church growth.[10] Western readers find difficulty in understanding how such movements can occur, and easily class them as primitive behaviour of people incapable of self-determination. As we have already seen, secular Western worldview places great emphasis upon the individual rather than the group. Thus, individual decisions are both accepted and encouraged as being characteristic of a mature person. In other societies, the emphasis is upon the community and not the individual. In these cases people are much more conscious of the feelings and reactions of the community with regards to their personal decisions. They therefore prefer to make decisions in line with the consensus of the whole community rather than out of personal preference.

In these cases the views and feelings of the individual are secondary to that of the community. An individual may have a new idea, but unless the community is ripe for the idea no change will occur. The study of culture change reveals that societies do reach points of time propitious for major change. Hegel's ideas may well have been laughed to scorn a hundred years earlier, but the changes which had occurred within the society made it ready to accept the new concepts in the 1820s. The harvest metaphor is one commonly used in the Bible, and it does indeed seem that God brings societies to those points of crises when they are ripe for decision. The right time comes for a major decision, but it is also possible that the opportunity may be lost.

Syncretism

Conversion and acculturation are never complete. People may embrace new ideas in dramatic movements, but they always bring with them parts of their past. The new ideas are often stated in terms of their old paradigms. The result is a strange mixing of ideas, new and old expressing themselves in an indigenous system of belief. Often it has occurred through the fanatical proselytising of the major world religions amongst primal societies.

The Spanish conquest of the New World in the early part of the sixteenth century was to produce radical changes amongst the indigenous people. The military superiority of the Spaniards was so pronounced that small armies numbering a few hundred were able to vanquish well-organised Aztec armies of thousands. The existing political organisations were either completely replaced or radically transformed. Roman Catholic missionaries travelled with every Spanish and Portuguese ship. They razed the temples and replaced them by Christian churches. The people accepted the new religion with its new names for the gods and new rituals of power, but these merely fitted into their traditional worldview.

Beneath the veneer of Roman Catholicism one finds in Mexico there are still the manifestations of the traditional religions.

> I saw devotees (whose devotion I do not doubt) crossing a cement plaza on their knees to a shrine more Aztec than Christian, while others put paper or cloth under their bloodstained knees to get it charged with power for magical and healing purposes; vendors selling magical herbs whose efficacy came from the blessings of the saints rather than any medical property, and this on the steps of the church; worshippers carrying shrines of straw and corn in some way after the manner of an old fertility cult; and a stream of persons one by one kissing away the toe of a stone statue to obtain thereby blessing on their lives and household; and all this was done in the name of Christianity.[11]

In pre-Columbian times, the main deities were the sun and the moon, who had a son – the 'god of the dead'. It was therefore a matter of little difficulty to equate the Virgin Mary with the moon deity, the traditional symbol of fertility and blessing, God with the sun, and the crucified Christ with their traditional god of the dead. The Roman Catholic custom of attaching saints' names to places, churches and shrines had its equivalent in traditional culture. The spirits of the ancient religion were also ascribed shrines, and so a mere transference of names was all that was needed.

Colonial legislation against primal religious beliefs has caused many issues to be hidden within the society. Laws made against witchcraft in Africa show an appalling ignorance of its place in the local culture. There should at least have been the acknowledgment of the difference between a witch and a witch doctor as the measure of their social guilt is not equal. The result was that these issues were not openly discussed, but they continued to be believed within the society.

People may therefore adhere to a new religion, or philosophy, and yet perceive those new ideas within the terms of their traditional worldview. The new religion is no more than a veneer. One finds this is the Muslim world where most would strongly affirm to be Muslims, but they would deviate markedly from the theology proposed by the scholar from a leading Islamic school of theology. In this way 'folk' religion is found in all the major world religions, including Christianity.

Syncretism has been defined as 'the union of two opposite forces, beliefs, systems or tenets so that the united form is a new thing, neither one nor the other'.[12] It can, however, be observed that there may be a variety of forms of mixing the cultural elements.

It is first necessary to make a distinction between the cultural 'form' and the 'meaning' of that form to the people of the society. The 'form' is simply defined as a cultural element which is seen and practised. At a deeper level are the ideas, or paradigms which are associated with the particular forms. For example, a golden ring worn on the third figure of the left hand is a cultural 'form', and has the 'meaning', within Western culture, that the person is married. Within another culture, that form of a wedding ring may not have the same meaning. It may merely mean that the person is wealthy, and likes to display their wealth.

The first pattern of syncretism is where the forms are changed to those advocated by the new culture whilst traditional ideological principles are retained. This is the pattern referred to in the conversion of the Central American people to Roman Catholicism. Christian names were given to traditional gods and rituals. It is always easier for an outward form to be communicated rather than some complex ideology. People will therefore accept a new religious ritual more readily than a new philosophy. This is seen in the case of the worldwide 'diffusion' of Coca-Cola which contrasts with the much slower diffusion of Christianity.

In the second pattern, the ideological concepts are accepted and local indigenous forms are used to express the ideas. This could be the singing of, say, a Western evangelical theology to the chant of a drumbeat previously used for traditional dancing. Luzbetak has called this 'accommodation', which he defines as, 'the respectful, prudent, scientifically and theologically sound adjustment of the Church to the native culture in attitude, outward behaviour, and practical apostolic approach'.[13] More recently the term 'indigenous' has been used.

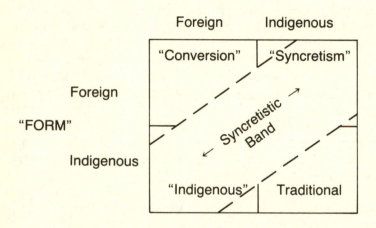

Figure 8.2 Relationship between form/meaning in culture

Figure 8.2 shows the possible relationships between form/ meaning and culture. It also shows the two other combinations which are possible. One is the acceptance of both the foreign form and the foreign ideology, and this we have called cultural conversion. The other, is the rejection of both the ideology and the form which, of course, means no change at all.

The form/meaning analysis can also be helpful in understanding contemporary Western issues. Take for example the question of whether Christians should be vegetarians. The form is the abstinence of eating meat. The meaning for a particular person may be determined by the answer to the question, why does one not eat meat? There could be several answers to this question.

First, meat is expensive and the person cannot afford meat. Secondly, the person considers that it is more healthy to avoid eating meat. Thirdly, there are those people who are concerned for the well-being of animals, and would try to avoid their ill-treatment and slaughter. Finally, there are those people, such as many Hindus, who would not eat meat because they believe in reincarnation and *karma*. A Christian, for example, may consider the first three reasons as acceptable, but the fourth as not being valid for them. The distinction between form and meaning can enable a Christian to make a personal value judgement as to the acceptability or not of a particular cultural form. This will become of increasing importance as worldviews interact causing the formation of a multitude of syncretistic religious movements.

In practice the division between acceptable and unacceptable syncretism is not as simple as it may appear from theoretical discussions. Christians from the same culture may come to differing views as to the validity of the meanings of a cultural form from their personal study of the Bible. Sometimes a cultural form may be adopted which disturbs the consciences of some other Christians. This is the problem of the 'weaker brother' of whom Paul writes in connection with meat which has been offered to idols (1 Cor 8:1–13). Paul himself had the liberty of conscience to eat meat even though he knew that there could have been the possibility of it having been offered to an idol as a sacrifice. However, for the sake of Gentile converts for whom this type of sacrifice had been an important element of their religious life, Paul refrained when it would cause misunderstanding and offence. 'The principle still applies today. Scripture takes conscience seriously and tells us not to violate it. It needs to be educated in order to become "strong", but while it remains "weak" it must be respected. A strong conscience will give freedom; but love limits liberty.'[14]

The problem becomes even more complex in a cross-cultural situation. As we saw with regard to the example of the wedding ring, two cultures may have very different meanings of the same form. However, the analysis of form and meaning does enable Christians to express their Christian beliefs in terms of their local cultural context.

Robert Ramseyer has shown the need for caution with regard to taking the form/meaning analysis to extremes.[15] The model was built from an analogy with language where the relationship between sounds and meaning are usually arbitrary. It implies that a sound (form) is always neutral carrying whatever meaning is given it by the culture. This assumption leads to two dangers. First, Christian mission is seen as 'primarily the transformation of the conceptual system (worldview) of that culture'.[16] This intellectual approach is characteristic of the Western Christian tradition, but fails to address questions of Christianity's behaviour. Secondly, if all forms are neutral how does one explain the nature of magic. Practitioners of magic are aware that it is through the correct practice of a ritual and utterance of specific words that power is liberated. This can be further illustrated by considering the Lord's Supper. Zwingli considered this to be no more than a symbolic act, whilst Calvin, and most Reformed theologians considered it to be 'a means of grace' by which spiritual blessing is mediated to the partaker. To assume that all forms are neutral is in practice applying a secular paradigm which is useful, but does have limitations.

We have so far considered three of Tippett's categories: demoralisation, conversion, and syncretism. The fourth is revitalisation which, in the next chapter, will draw upon many of the issues which we have just been describing to produce a new paradigm and culture in the form of a new religious movement.

Notes

1. Schaeffer, Francis. *The God who is There* (Hodder & Stoughton: London, 1968) p 14.
2. Linton, Ralph. *The Study of Man* (D. Appleton-Century Company: New York, 1936) p 325.
3. Wallace, Anthony F.C. *Religion: An Anthropological View* (Random House: New York, 1966).
4. Tippett, Alan. *Introduction to Missiology* (William Carey Library: Pasadena, 1987) pp 157–182.
5. Tippett, *ibid* p 163.
6. Davies, David. *The Last of the Tasmanians* (Frederick Muller: London, 1973).
7. Personal comments from Ivan Lowe.
8. Walsh, Brian J. and Middleton, J. Richard. *The Transforming Vision* (IVP: Downes Grove, 1984) p 24.
9. Benthall, Jonathan. 'The Anthropology of Tourism', *Anthropology Today* Vol. 4 No. 3 June 1988, pp 20–22.
10. McGavran, Donald. *Understanding Church Growth* (Eerdmans: Grand Rapids, 1970) pp 296–333.
11. Tippett, *op cit*, p 173.
12. Yamamori, Tetsunao and Taber, Charles R. *Christopaganism or Indigenous Christianity?* (William Carey Library: Pasadena, 1975) p 17.
13. Luzbetak, Louis J. *The Church and Cultures* (Divine Word Publications: Techny, 1970) p 341.
14. *The Willowbank Report – Gospel and Culture* (Lausanne Committee for World Evangelisation: Wheaton, 1978) p 29.
15. Ramseyer, Robert L. 'Christian Mission and Cultural Anthropology' in Wilbert R. Shenk, *Exploring Church Growth* (Eerdman: Grand Rapids, 1983) pp 113–115.
16. Kraft, Charles H. *Christianity and Culture* (Orbis Books: Maryknoll, 1979) p 349.

9

NEW RELIGIOUS MOVEMENTS

In the previous chapter, we considered three patterns of worldview change: demoralisation, conversion, syncretism. We will now turn to the fourth pattern referred to which was revitalisation movements, or more popularly known as 'new religious movements'. It is all too easy for Christians to disregard these movements as small insignificant sects whereas the scope of such movements is worldwide. 'With more than 10,000 different new religious movements in Africa, 500 in the USA, 450 in Germany, 95 in the United Kingdom, and similar numbers in other parts of the world, we are faced with an almost endless variety of movements.'[1]

The fact of the variety of such movements makes classification almost impossible, but one can identify certain common types of these movements. Although one can recognise the danger of over-simplification, we are here going to class these religious movements into three types.

1)   New religious movements emerging as a result of contact of a major world religion (with its culture) and a primal society. By far the most common form are those which have occurred between Christianity and primal societies. Thousands of such movements have emerged through the expansion of the European peoples.

2)   New religious movements emerging out of a general dissatisfaction with the traditional expression of the world religion. The new form of religion would still regard itself as being Christian, Muslim, Hindu etc, but it is usually regarded as an unacceptable expression of that religion by the main

exponents. The Jehovah's Witnesses would be a Christian example, and the Ahmadiyya a Muslim example.

3) New religious movements resulting from the importation of ideas and rituals from another dominant culture. The result is a syncretistic interpretation of the ideas and rituals often with the establishment of a new life-style. The Hara Krishna movement in the West would illustrate such a movement.

In this chapter, we are aiming to examine firstly the reason for and dynamics of the growth of such new religious movements, and secondly to examine the first of our three categories which are those emerging from primal societies.

Stages in a revitalisation movement

Wallace was one of the first to describe the patterns by which successful revitalisation movements developed.[2] He showed that in all these cases the exponents of the particular movement are seeking to formulate a more satisfactory worldview.

Stage one. Initially the culture is in steady-state experiencing relatively slow and essentially undisruptive change. The stress levels vary amongst individuals within the society, but are generally tolerable and acceptable.

Stage two. As a result of contact with a dominant foreign culture, climatic change, epidemic, or war, the society is thrown out of equilibrium. An increasing number of individuals are placed under what to them is intolerable stress by the failure of the system to meet their needs. Often demoralisation and sickness increase in frequency, but the situation is still considered to be no more than a fluctuation in the steady-state.

Stage three. Some members of the society attempt minor changes to the system, but they are usually ineffective and only increase the social tension. Alcoholism, crime, and failure to obey the traditional leadership all increase. The established patterns of social behaviour are rejected by particular sub-groups usually the young. Some groups lose confidence in the value of maintaining social cohesion and may resort to violence in order to take advantage of the situation.

Stage four. Once severe cultural stress has occurred, it is difficult for the society to return to its previous steady-state. The society may disintegrate through demoralisation as discussed in the previous chapter, but there is also the possibility of a revitalisation process. From out of the social upheaval comes a prophetic figure who in a desire to find answers to his own situation has a revelation which allows the formulation of a new structure for society. Usually there is the promise of a new world which will emerge out of the pain of the present disaster. There will be no more sickness, no more poverty or oppression. A new world order will be imposed from above – a millennium.

Stage five. The acceptance of the new movement with its new worldview provides a more satisfactory answer to the people's needs. Individual stress is reduced, new leadership emerges, and new patterns of behaviour develop. Although the culture will continue to undergo change this will be modifications of the new steady-state formulation.

Many attempts at revitalisation may occur, but for one to succeed it is necessary for it to have the following characteristics.

First, there is the need for the formulation of a new pattern for the future which will provide the basis of a new worldview. This most commonly occurs through a religious revelation to an individual. It may reveal to him a new god who is calling him to a mission to save his people. It may be the expectation of the imminent coming of a new heaven and earth free of sickness, and salvation which will come through a new ritual.

Non-religious formulations are rare, but do occur in politically oriented movements. Some individuals have known a conversion to Marxist philosophy which is akin to a religious conversion. They have received a new perception of the economic and social world, and a new vision of a classless society. One may also add that they have a new text in *Das Kapital*, and the *Communist Manifesto*.

Secondly, the new vision must be communicated to others with evangelistic zeal. Unless converts are made, the vision will die with the visionary, and no record of the movement be known. The vision is a means of salvation for the people, and it is usually brought by the 'prophet' with a deep conviction and sincerity. It will usually be preached, but will often be accompanied by some new symbolism of the message. The prophet will maybe wear a white robe signifying a new righteousness, or cut his hair in a new way, or carry a staff as a mark of his new authority. He, or she, will stand out as a demonstration of the new hope for society.

In small societies, the message of the prophet is directed to the entire community. The revelation is for the whole of the tribe, and comes to meet their particular felt-needs. In more complex societies, the message may be aimed only at certain groups deemed eligible for the new society. Often the enquirer is told that he will be misunderstood and even persecuted by the unbelievers in the world.

Thirdly, as the movement attracts converts there is a need to develop patterns of leaders and organisation. Where these are lacking one may find a small group of forty or fifty followers associated with their particular prophet. Amongst the independent churches of Africa one frequently finds a prophet, often an illiterate woman, who has established a little church with a few followers. She is able to meet the needs for the little group, but lacks the organisation for further growth. It is like a person who runs a little shop able to meet the needs of a limited number of customers. However, some shop-keepers may realise that if they appoint someone to run the first shop they could open a second. Once this has been achieved, what is to stop them from opening a third, fourth, fifth – an unlimited number. The same may happen with the prophet and his followers as a complex administrative structure is developed for the propagation of the new religion.

As the group of converts expands, it tends to divide into two parts: the committed disciples and the followers. The disciples are those who have had a conversion experience parallel to that of the prophet, and thus develop a loyalty and commitment to him. They increasingly become part of the executive organisa-

tion, responsible for administering the evangelistic programme, developing theology, combating heresy, organising
rituals, and acquiring money for the movement. The disciples
may become full-time workers for the organisation being sup-
ported by the masses of followers. They may join communes
focused around the prophet with the aim of establishing the
new order in the world today. The followers, on the other
hand, continue in their roles in the existing culture devoting
part of their time and money to the movement.

The prophet may be so revered by his dedicated disciples
that he is elevated to such a degree that he is considered to be
superhuman, and even a god. Take for example, Shri Guru
Maharaj Ji of the Divine Light. It is written in their magazines
of the 1970s: 'Wherever Guru Maharaj Ji appears, His
devotees flock to see Him and to touch His Lotus Feet. They
shower Him with tokens of their love, because He is their Lord
and Creator in human form and has given them True Knowledge.'[3] This is not only flattering for the prophet who may
come to sincerely believe he has this status, but gives greater
authority to his teaching and greater commitment to his followers. This allows the movement to attract more followers as the
mystique of the prophet grows, and it also has the additional
value of attracting more finance.

Fourthly, the first visions of the prophet may provide a basis
of an answer to the societies, but they need to be developed to
achieve a more comprehensive worldview. Inadequacies are
constantly being found in the existing culture, and failures and
ambiguities are discovered within the new religion itself. The
latter are often pointed out by those opposed to the movement.
The teaching of the movement therefore is gradually reworked
until it provides a satisfactory answer to a wide variety of issues.

Finally, the movement needs to generate a new life-style that
can provide for the basic needs of the people. In a small society,
the movement may capture the adherence of the whole tribe,
and the new religion and culture become accepted. One can see
this most remarkably with the Arabs' acceptance of Islam in the
seventh century. The revelations of the prophet Muhammad

after a period of rejection were accepted by all the Arab tribes. This not only united the various factions, but revitalised them into a community with a new religion, mission and life-style.

It should be noted that some new religious movements, such as Islam, break out of the culture which gave them birth. These religions tend to have a monistic or monotheistic worldview, and therefore consider their religion as being relevant and significant to all humanity. The resulting missionary zeal may well transform the new tribal religion into a world religion. Christianity, Buddhism, and even Communism may be considered as being born out of such revitalisation movements.

From this theoretical discussion we want to turn to examine the first of the three classes of new religious movements. These are new movements originating from within primal societies and occurring from contact with a major world religion which in most cases is European Christianity.

Movements occurring within primal societies

We have already pointed out that with the European expansion many tribal societies were placed under great social stress. This has lead to the demoralisation and disintegration of many small societies. In other cases there has been a reworking of the old traditions in the light of contact with the new dominant culture and religion. Harold Turner has defined these movements in the following way, 'A historically new development arising from the interaction between a primal society and its religion and another culture and its major religion, and involving some substantial departure from the classical religious traditions of both the cultures concerned in order to find renewal by reworking the rejected traditions into a different religious system'.[4]

The earliest recorded movement amongst primal societies appeared in Guatemala in 1530, soon after interaction with the Christianity carried by the Spaniards. Since that time hundreds of similar religious movements have occurred throughout the world (see Figure 9.1).

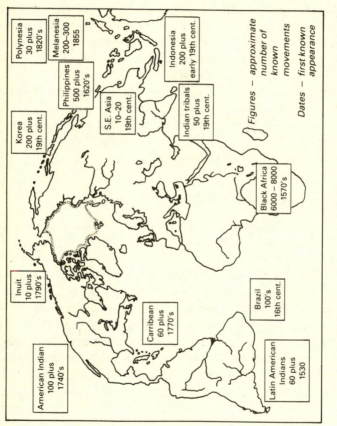

Figure 9.1 New Religious Movements amongst primal societies
Harold Turner (1984)

Inuit
10 plus
1790's

American Indian
100 plus
1740's

Carribean
60 plus
1770's

Brazil
100's
16th cent.

Latin American
Indians
60 plus
1530

Korea
200 plus
19th cent.

Philippines
500 plus
1620's

Polynesia
30 plus
1820's

Melanesia
200–300
1855

S.E. Asia
10–20
19th cent.

Indonesia
200 plus
early 19th cent.

Indian tribals
50 plus
19th cent.

Black Africa
6000 – 8000
1570's

Figures – approximate
number of
known
movements

Dates – first known
appearance

North America

A classic American example of a revitalisation movement was the Ghost Dance of 1890 among the Plains Indians of the United States. The buffalo which had been the mainstay of the Plains Indians' way of life had finally been destroyed by the white men. The Indians were being herded into reservations. It seemed as if the independent life of the Plains Indians had come to an end.

A young man called Wovoka was taken by David Wilson to work on his ranch. He was encouraged to join the family in daily prayers and Bible reading. Jack, as Wovoka became known, became good friends with the family, but he never lost his pride in his own Paiute people. Jack married a Paiute girl and they set up home as a respected young couple in the Mason Valley community.

It was on 1 January 1889, whilst Wovoka lay sick on his bed, that a momentous happening occurred. A dramatic total eclipse of the sun occurred over the land. The Indians shot off guns to frighten away the monstrous force overcoming the sun. Wovoka felt himself losing consciousness. It seemed as though he was taken up to heaven and brought before God. God gave him a message for the people of earth, and then both he and the sun regained their normal life. Wovoka was now a prophet.

The writer Mooney, to whom he once told his story, recounts:

He saw God, with all the people who had died long ago engaged in their old time sports and occupations, all happy and forever young. It was a pleasant land and full of game. After showing him all, God told him he must go back and tell his people they must be good and love one another, have no quarrelling, and live in peace with the whites; that they must work, and not lie or steal; that they must put away all the old practices that savoured of war; that if they faithfully obeyed his instructions they would at last be reunited with the friends in the old world, where there would be no more death or sickness or old age. He was then given the dance which he was commanded to bring back to his people. By performing this dance at intervals, for five consecutive days each time, they would secure this happiness to themselves and hasten the event. Finally God gave him control over the elements so that he could make it rain or snow or to be dry at will, and appointed his deputy to take charge of affairs in the west, while 'Governor Harrison' (President of the United States at the time) would attend to matters in the east, and he, God, would look after the world above.[5]

This was a religion for all people, but Wovoka knew that it was of no value to preach to the white men who were more interested in the land. It was a marvellous message for people suffering as were the Plains Indians in 1889 with terrible epidemics, loss of land and malnutrition. It provided them with a circling dance which pleased their senses, and offered emotional experiences during their long rituals. The religion was quickly taken up by his own people the Paiute, and it spread to the Cheyenne, Pawnee, Wichita, Sioux, and many of the other Plains Indians.

The white settlers became frightened by what they called the 'Ghost Dance', and the US Army was brought in because they suspected an armed uprising. Some of the Wovoka followers did not fully appreciate his message of peace, and some of the movement's leaders amongst the Sioux Indians introduced a special shirt which was claimed no bullet would go through. The short rebellion was quickly put down by the US Cavalry at the 'Massacre of Wounded Knee', 1890.

The failure of the movement led to the disintegration of the Indian society. Some of the people turned to drink, others to hallucinogenic drugs in an effort to hide from the reality about them. Only with the recent growth of the 'Red Power' movement has there been the sense of renewal amongst this dispirited people. Amidst this demoralisation has remained the recorded life of Black Elk, a visionary of the Oglala Sioux. It was in 1971 that the book *Black Elk Speaks* suddenly became a cult book in the States.[6] It is a strange twist to the story that the visions of an old Indian shaman have become popular amongst a new generation of white Americans, and on 29 December 1990 many people across the world will gather to commemorate the centenary of the massacre at Wounded Knee. The villains of one worldview are often the heroes of another.

Pacific

From Tanna in the New Hebrides comes an example of a revitalisation movement typical of the Pacific Islands. Tanna was first contacted by a white man in 1774 when it was visited by Captain Cook. It was in 1869 that a Christian mission was established by British Presbyterians. By 1920 the island was effectively Christianised with an estimated 4,000 Christians and 1,000 'heathens'.

Today the island is dotted with many wooden crosses in their fenced gardens. The followers of this new religion are waiting for the return of a mysterious man whom they call John Frum. This enigmatic person appeared shortly before World War II bringing a message of freedom and claiming to be the reincarnation of Karapenmun, a former god of Tanna. John Frum went away, though from time to time he spoke through certain leaders who would then pass his messages on to the people.

During World War II, the American troops landed on the islands with unlimited types of Western goods, from rifles to washing machines, cigarettes to candy bars. These were luxuries undreamed of by a stone-age people. One only had to look at these items to see that they had not been chipped, or woven as were familiar to the people of Tanna. The conclusion was that this cargo must have come from John Frum, and should be repossessed by force. The movement has endured seventeen years of mass arrests, deportations, and imprisonments by the British. The Frumist leaders believe that John Frum will return with cargo and with a better life for the people of Tanna. He will expel their white rulers, and once again Tanna will take its place as the centre of the universe and the island will be restored to its former glory.[7]

Similar movements have occurred in the Solomon Islands, and amongst the Maori of New Zealand.[8] Usually the prophet has been a real man who has remained with his people, but the belief in a new age to come and 'cargo' has been common to many in the Pacific.

Cargo cults such as the John Frum movement are a direct result of culture contact with Westerners. The new religious movement provides answers to the two major disruptions that have come to their society: Christian missionaries and traders with Western goods. Christian missionaries condemned the ancient gods as devils, and reverence for the ancestors was ridiculed. Traders introduced Western goods to the islands. It is easy to imagine the reaction of 'stone-age' natives to their first sight of planes, radios, and canned food. The native could not conceive of how these items could be made by humans, and therefore came to the conclusion that these are goods from the ancestors. In the case of the John Frum cult, the followers constructed a dummy landing strip in preparation for the arrival of the aircraft bringing the cargo.

Africa

It is in Africa that one finds the greatest number of such movements. With the coming of the Western missionary the first response of many African people was that of acceptance and conversion to the new religion. Western schools and hospitals all encouraged the process of cultural conversion. However, Western missionaries were often unaware of some of the deep problems left unresolved in the hearts of people holding previously to a primal worldview. How will the ancestors react to a person becoming a Christian? How can one deal with witches and spirits? How does one find out when to plant one's crops? The new religion seemed to have no equivalent answers to these questions as compared to the answers given by the traditional worldview.

Then there was the question of the land. The white man came first to trade, but soon he started taking the land and expanding his colonial rule. He started to bring in his foreign legal systems, and started to grow crops for export. He needed migrant labour to work in the fields, and this took the young men away from their traditional homelands. As Chinua

Achebe entitles his book, *Things Fall Apart*.[9] The African societies struggle to find their new identities within the rapidly changing world.

David Barrett has said that there is often 'an incubation period averaging sixty years' after the coming of the first Western missionary before the emergence of new religious movements.[10] A prophet usually emerges from the situation of stress and confusion with a new message for the people's needs. These are usually called 'African Independent Churches' because they were initiated by Africans; they are usually breakaway movements from established missionary churches, and they claim to be Christian.

Although the movements would call themselves Christian, in all cases there is a considerable degree of syncretism. At one extreme are those movements which seem to have little resemblance to Christianity in other parts of the world. They may have adopted some Christian symbols such as a cross, or white robes, but essentially their worldview is primal, and not biblical. At the other extreme are those movements who have a biblical worldview, but are expressing it in ways which are typically African. They do not just stand to sing Christian hymns, but show their enthusiasm in dance and clapping. These movements stretch from unacceptable syncretism to the application of acceptable indigenous African forms for Christian worship.

China

These movements have also grown in sophisticated societies such as the Chinese of the nineteenth century. The most notable was that which issued in the Taiping Rebellion of 1851-1864. This movement shook the Chinese Empire to the core in its attempt to reform Chinese society, not in terms of traditional Chinese thinking, but according to Protestant Christianity. The Taiping Rebellion drew worldwide attention and sympathy from Christians. Here were simple Chinese peasants taking ideas from the Bible, and applying them to bring a new social order to China.

The Taiping Rebellion illustrates the usual pattern of social stress, prophetic figure, and syncretism. China of 1850 was under stress from many quarters. The Chinese people resented the misrule of the alien Manchu overlords, European nations were penetrating into the land, and over-population was placing additional burden on food production. The attempts of the government to shore up the sagging regime merely exacerbated the problems. The situation was fertile ground for the emergence of a prophet.

Hung Hsiu-chuan was a Hakka born in 1814 about thirty miles from Canton. He came from a peasant family who worked hard so that he could study to gain academic qualifications. At sixteen he tried to pass prefectural exams, but he failed as he did on two following occasions. During the times of his examinations he heard a foreign evangelist preaching and received a set of nine tracts. He payed little attention to these. After failing for a third time, Hung had a nervous breakdown. It was during this time that Hung claimed to have had visions, one which took him to heaven, where he appeared before a venerable old man who identified himself as the creator. The old man complained to Hung about two things: the widespread worship of demons and the fact that Confucius had failed to teach the true doctrine. In another vision, Hung met a middle-aged man, whom he called his Elder Brother. This man, whom he later claimed was Jesus Christ, instructed him on how to kill demons. God commissioned Hung, his second son, to go into the world and bring China back to the worship of the true God.

Hung heard of the doctrine of baptism and in 1843 baptised his cousin who in turn baptised him. Hung was finally expelled from his village for destroying Confucian tablets. As the number of converts increased the group became known as 'Pai Shang Ti Hui' (God-worshippers). As banditry increased in the area the group organised themselves into a disciplined military force. New visions were given and those who died in battle were claimed to go directly to heaven.

Their first clash with the government forces was singularly successful, and they celebrated the victory with a public ceremony of prayer and thanksgiving. In March 1853, they conquered Nanking, and then many other cities of the region. The Taiping ranks swelled from a ragged band, to several thousands, and finally to more than one million disciplined troops. The movement was however plagued with dissent which led to the murder of some of the army commanders. The Taiping threat to traditional Chinese thought led to loyal Chinese joining the Government forces to quell the rebellion. By July 1864, the Taipings had been reduced to the control of only the city of Nanking which was surrounded. Hung refused to flee and committed suicide. It is estimated that the Taiping rebellion took twenty million lives,[11] and radically changed the history of China.

Missionaries initially had little contact with the movement, but when they finally did they were appalled. 'The rebels were resorting to violence. The Scriptures they applied were misinterpreted, distorted, taken out of context; these revolutionaries were submitting not to God but to their visible leader, Hung Hsiu-chuan, who claimed to be a younger brother of Jesus and recipient of direct revelations from God.'[12]

The movement was a curious blend of Christian and Confucian ideas.[13] It insisted upon reverence for God, but stressed filial piety. Jesus was the Son of God, but Hung was the second son who had received a new heavenly mandate. They preached the brotherhood of all men, but also held to social hierarchy in which the ancient practices of *li* were important. They offered animal sacrifices to God, but not the traditional Chinese offerings of rice, tea or wine. They observed baptism and the Sabbath, but used flags as a symbol and not the cross. Several Taoist and Buddhist elements were incorporated into their ceremonies such as the use of drums, firecrackers, and cakes.

The distinctive Christian ideas accepted by the Taiping were the respect for and equality of women, and acceptance of monogamy. It was as a result of this that many women fought in the Taiping Rebellion. Another concept was a communal type of lifestyle especially related to the use of land. However, Christ's teaching about forgiveness, humility and love for one another were omitted. If the Golden Rule had been accepted maybe the violence and destruction would not have occurred.

New religious movements bring new dreams, but not all succeed. Many hopes blow away with the winds of time as the prophet fails to meet the expectations of his followers. The clash of worlds requires new models of reality, and this applies to Western man as well as primal man or the peasants of nineteenth-century China. We must therefore now turn to the great civilisations of the world to look at the growth of new movements of human religious creativity.

Notes

1. LCWE *Christian Witness to New Religious Movements* (LCWE: Illinois, 1980) p 5.
2. Wallace, Anthony F.C. *Religion: An Anthropological View* (Random House: New York, 1966) pp 158–166.
3. *Divine Light Magazine* Vol 3, No 3 (1973) p 1.
4. Turner, Harold. 'Tribal Religious Movements, New' in *Encyclopaedia Britannica* (Encyclopaedia Britannica Ltd: Chicago, 1981), Vol 18, p 698.
5. Kehoe, Alice Beck. *The Ghost Dance: Ethnohistory and Revitalization* (Holt, Reinhart and Winston: New York, 1989) p 6.
6. Neihardt, John G. *Black Elk Speaks* (Washington Square Press: New York, 1971).
7. Rice, Edward. *John Frum He Come* (Doubleday & Company: New York, 1974).
8. Tippett, Allan. *Solomon Islands Christianity* (William Carey Library: Pasadena, 1967).
9. Achebe, Chinua. *Things Fall Apart* (Heinemann: London, 1976).
10. Barrett, David B. *Schism and Renewal in Africa* (Oxford University Press: Nairobi, 1968) p 139.
11. 'Taiping Rebellion', in *Encyclopaedia Britannica* (Encyclopaedia Britannica: Chicago, 1981), Micropaedia, Vol IX, p 774.
12. Corwin, Charles. *East to Eden?* (Eerdmans Publishing Co.: Grand Rapids, 1972) p 67.
13. Boardman, Eugene P. 'Millenary Aspects of the Taiping Rebellion (1851–64)' in *Millennial Dreams in Action* Ed. Sylvia L. Thrupp (Mounton: The Hague, 1962), pp 70–79.

10

SECTS AND CULTS:
New religious movements II

Readers of *The Gazette* in Scotia, New York on 12 November 1970 saw this advertisement:

> The world has entered a new stage of history, the age of the maturity of man and the beginning of the world civilisation. The source of this new development was a Man who was exiled, tortured, banished and imprisoned for more than 40 years. He lived during the last century. His name: BAHA'U'LLAH – THE GLORY OF GOD. Baha'u'llah is the latest in the succession of Divine Messengers sent by God since the beginning of man's existence. He is the Promised One of all religions. His coming ushers in the Age of Fulfilment ... Baha'u'llah brings God's Plan for world peace, world justice and world unity.

New religious movements have not merely arisen from primal societies, but also from within the dominant cultures of East and West. As mentioned in the previous chapter we are going to classify these into two general types:

1) New movements emerging from within a world religion, and still claiming to be part of that religious tradition.
2) New movements emerging out of the deliberate importation of ideas and concepts of another culture or world religion.

This classification is very similar to that proposed by Harold Turner where he calls these 'sects' and 'cults' respectively.[1]

Recognising that these terms have their limitations, they do at least provide us with a framework in which to discuss the issues. We might therefore accept Reinhart Hummel's comment, 'Here sects are seen, roughly speaking, as deviant movements derived from mainstream (in the West, Christianity) religion, whereas cults are deviant movements outside mainstream religion, either imported from outside or originated outside mainstream religion.'[2] One would therefore class Jehovah's Witnesses, Christian Scientists, and the Children of God in the first category, and the Hara Krishna, Baha'i, and Divine Light Movement in the second.

Sects

H. Richard Niebuhr suggested that all religious movements started life as sects amongst the poor, oppressed and under-privileged.[3] This class felt themselves alienated from the values of the dominant social order of society. The poor therefore fashion for themselves a religion which meets their social needs, and expresses their particular aspirations. Thus, sects are reform movements that emphasise certain elements within the tradition of the established religion while rejecting other elements.

Jehovah's Witnesses concentrate on those elements of biblical teaching relating to the Second coming and the end of the world. The evil condition of the world is the result of man's disobedience to the will of God. They consider that there is no way that the conditions on earth can be improved by humans, but God personally will take over the government of the world and create a new earth. Those people who live in adherence to the teachings of the *Watch Tower* will survive to live on the new earth. Jehovah's Witnesses therefore reject all earthly authorities of whatever political persuasion. They do not reject the use of technology, but do refuse those aspects of science which question a literalist reading of the Bible.

Niebuhr argued that sects grow through the active proselytisation of their members. As the sect grows in age, an increasing percentage of those joining the group are children of members.

A large proportion of the second generation are therefore not converted from 'unbelief', but have been raised from birth to become members of the sect. The encouragement of inter-group marriage means that the movement takes on many of the characteristics of a distinct social group.

With time, the members of the group, through mutual co-operation, hard work, frugality and moderation become more wealthy. This is the process known in Church Growth circles as 'Redemption-and-Lift'. The enthusiasm of the younger gener-ation for the strict teaching of the founders tends to wane. The practices and beliefs of the group therefore become more acceptable to the larger community, and the movement finally becomes recognised as a denomination amongst other accepted denominations.

Niebuhr was primarily concerned with those movements such as Methodism and Pentecostalism which have been well researched. However, it is necessary to state that not all sects have been accepted by the larger community, and some have been positively rejected as we shall see. In popular thinking a sect is regarded as a movement which has not been accepted by the wider community and retains its own distinct identity.

Recognising the limitations of the model, it does have value for the study of sects not only from the Christian tradition, but also those from other world religions. As with new religious movements from primal societies, one finds the situation of stress, the rise of a prophetic figure, and a syncretism of material to establish a more satisfactory worldview.

Christian Sects

Many new religious movements developed from within the North American Church especially in the nineteenth century. Almost all have had a very strong missionary emphasis, and have moved out from North America to many countries of the world. These movements seem to arise out of an attempt to make European Christianity relevant to the New World. In some cases, this required an answer to the question, 'Who were the original Americans?'

The Utah-based Church of the Latter-day Saints provides one of the most striking examples. *Christianity Today*, May 1976 reported the 1975 world membership of this movement as 3,570,000 with a 50% growth over a ten-year period.[4] Today approximately one out of every one hundred US citizens is a Mormon. In Britain, they have grown from 70,000 in 1970, to 80,000 in 1975 and 102,000 in 1985.

Joseph Smith, the founder of the Mormon movement, shows many of the characteristics common to a prophet-type. Joseph Smith was a young man when his family moved from Vermont to New York. He claimed that in the spring of 1820 he went out into the woods to pray for wisdom concerning church membership. At that time, he claimed that God the Father and Jesus Christ appeared to him as two separate and distinct persons. He was told not to join any church for they were all wrong, and their creeds corrupt.

Then, in 1823, an angel appeared to Joseph to tell him of an ancient record hid in a nearby hill. The next day he uncovered the gold plates which contained the history of the former inhabitants of the continent, a people called Nephi. Smith also claims to have found Urim and Thummin with the plates which God had prepared for the purpose of translating this book.[5] The record claims that Christ visited the American continent, and revealed himself to the Nephites. He preached the gospel to them, instituted baptism, the communion service, the priesthood, and other mystical ceremonies. The Nephites were later destroyed by the Lamanite people in approximately AD 428. It needs to be stated that no archaeological evidence has ever been discovered to substantiate these views.[6]

Mormon theology has some remarkable differences from traditional Christianity. First, God is asserted to be a progressive being. He has not always been a god, but was once a man and developed into such a being through what he did. Secondly, each man has the potential to be god, and is in fact god in embryo. Thirdly, salvation is by works. All men will be saved (resurrected), but whatever one receives beyond this is as a result of the good works one does. Fourthly, to receive the fullness of exaltation a man must have a wife and a woman must have a husband. The couple must be sealed to each other for both time and eternity in a temple ceremony known as celestial marriage. Finally, it is believed that members must work for the salvation of the dead of their own lineage as far back as they can go.

The Church of Jesus Christ of Latter Day Saints was organised on 6th April 1830. It was presided over by Joseph Smith until his death. Settlers reacted strongly against the teachings of Smith and especially his claim to the land. Mobs began to attack Mormons, and Smith was imprisoned. On 27th June 1844 a mob attacked the jail holding Joseph Smith and hung him. Following his death there was a period of disintegration with the near collapse of the church. However, it was reorganised by Brigham Young and the Mormon community migrated westward to establish new headquarters in Salt Lake City, Utah.

The movement now has a well organised structure based upon two priesthoods – the Melchizedek and Aaronic. Every male member of the church who is over twelve years of age (except a Negro) has the opportunity of being ordained to some office in the priesthood, if he lives 'worthily'.[7] The Mormons have a strong sense of community, and a clear policy for mission with 23,000 missionaries.[8]

Christian Science, Jehovah's Witnesses, Christadelphianism and the Mormon Church all developed within the nineteenth century. These movements have changed since their foundation, but in general they have not been accepted by the orthodox Christian tradition. More recently there has been a wave of new movements which show many of Niebuhr's characteristics of a first generation sect.

The Children of God movement provides a more recent example. It was founded by David Berg, the son of a devout Christian couple who pastored a Missionary Alliance church in Virginia. Berg joined his mother in running a Teen Challenge coffee bar in the 1960s. It appears that it was here that his anti-establishment attitude took root. In 1969 he left the coffee bar with his wife and about fifty followers on trek to Arizona. They eventually settled at the Texas Soul Clinic Missionary Ranch where they stayed until growing criticism led to them being expelled by the owner. By this time, the Children of God numbered at least 2,000 and had sufficient resources to continue on their own.

David Berg was believed to have received direct revelations from God. Later these evolved into what became known as 'MO letters' considered to be God's inspired word for today. Sex became a central theme of the MO letters. Sexual licence gradually widened to homosexuality, advocation of childhood sex, and 'flirty fishing' by which female members were encouraged to offer their bodies as an inducement for men to join the organisation.[9] Berg's sexual philosophy which included wife-swapping was justified by the use of Acts 2:44, 'all things in common'.

At its peak, the Children of God had a membership of nearly 10,000 in 72 countries. Stories of their immorality, brainwashing, and corruption led to the disintegration of the group. The name of the sect was changed to the 'Family of Love' in 1978, and only a few hard core members remain.

Muslim Sects

Religious movements do not only occur from Christianised communities, but they also develop from within Islam as can be seen in the growth of the Ahmadiyya.

To understand the growth of the Ahmadiyya it is necessary to understand the insecurity sensed by Muslims in India during the latter part of the last century. They were outnumbered by Hindus who threatened to keep them permanently in subjection if the ruling British were to leave. Christian missionaries were also having a telling effect upon the thinking of the Indian people.

Mirza Ghulam Ahmad was born into a leading Muslim family of the Punjab in 1839. Although he tried to please his father by being involved in the family business, he seemed more prone to religious meditation. He is said to have had visions and dreams, and to have heard voices. Finally, he claimed to have received a special revelation from God that he would be the renewer of Islam at the beginning of the fourteenth Islamic century (AD 1882 was AH 1300). In 1889 he claimed the right to accept homage from his disciples.¹This drew the line of demarcation between the new sect and Islam. In 1974 the Government of Pakistan passed a law which essentially declared the Ahmadis to be a non-Muslim minority in the country.

Shortly before his death in 1908, Mirza Ahmad claimed 500,000 followers, but most observers would say that this was grossly inflated.[10] After Mirza Ahmad's death the movement passed into the hands of Hakim Nur-ud-Din, one of his disciples. He was an intelligent, industrious man who set up organisations for the administration and education of the community. The Ahmadis continued to grow despite persecution from the orthodox Muslims. The community migrated from Qadian to a barren area of land ninety miles southwest of Lahore which they sought to make habitable. Out of it has emerged the city of Rabwah with a strong centralised organisation. This well organised structure has made possible a vigorous missionary effort throughout the world. The Ahmadis can today boast of congregations in Europe and the United States, Africa and many parts of Asia.

Buddhist Sects

One of the world's most important sects grew from Hinduism, and has become a world religion in its own right. Siddartha Gautama was born around the year 500 BC, the son of the king of the Sakya tribe who lived in the foothills of the Himalayas. He showed no interest in religion until he reached the age of thirty when as a result of observing the poverty, sickness and death in society, turned towards considering the meaning and purpose of life. He abandoned his wife and child and set out as a poor pilgrim to seek an answer to the ultimate questions of life.

After some years of travelling around India visiting various gurus, he was left disillusioned. One day he sat down under a Bo tree determined not to leave the spot until he had achieved enlightenment. While sat under the tree he had a revelation which gave him an experience of liberation from *maya* and the achievement of Nirvana. His teachings had many of the worldview themes characteristic to Hinduism, and he himself spoke of the 'Middle Way' – an alternative path within the Hindu system.

Siddartha Gautama, now more commonly referred to as the Buddha, travelled throughout India teaching his new philosophy. He gathered around him a group of disciples who travelled with him. He also established a monastic order, the Sangha, which organised the subsequent converts in the many places he visited.

Gautama claimed to have discovered the 'Truth of Suffering' which is that all individual existence separate from the ultimate is suffering. It is desire which sustains the momentum of the endless cycles of transmigration. Thus, the way to end this cycle of suffering is to end desire. In this way the momentum of *karma* will be used up and the illusion of separate existence brought to an end, in realisation of Nirvana. The way to achieve this cessation of desire is to follow the discipline of the Eightfold Path which leads to the realisation of 'Non-self' and identification with the ultimate 'Self'.

Buddhism was in the first place a discipline rather than a religion, and consists of a rule of life rather than a system of worship. Ignorance of the teachings of Buddha means that people are condemned to the sorrow and suffering of endless rebirths, and thus provides a stimulus for the missionary outreach. In the third century BC, King Asoka, a devoted follower of the Buddha, encouraged the spread of Buddhism across much of Asia. Within each cultural group that it entered it took upon itself something of the traditional beliefs of the people. Today, Buddhism is one of the major religions of the world.

Cults

Whilst sects are reform movements within a world religion, cults reject the tradition in favour of another. During the twentieth century a multitude of new religious movements have come from an interaction between two or more of the universal faiths. This is as may be expected with the increasing communication and travel which has occurred in this century.

There are numerous ways in which cults may be classified, but we shall use the scheme of relating the movement to the major tradition from which it draws its inspiration. In general these have been those of a mystical nature.

Islam

The traditional hostility which has existed between Islam and Western Christianity has not encouraged much interaction between these traditions. However, there has been an increasing interest amongst Westerners in Sufism, the mystical aspects of Islam. This exposes once again the major weakness of the secular worldview in that it fails to provide an inner transcendental experience. Orthodox Islam does not provide for such a need, but Sufism does and so accounts for the Western converts to this practice.

Islam has, however, known those who have been influenced by other religions such as Christianity, and one example is the Bahai. Sayyid Ali Muhammad, better known as the Bab, was born in Shiraz, Iran, in 1820. As a young man he worked with his uncle's business. After a few years he left the work to pursue religious interests and on 23 May 1844 he made the historic declaration that he had been chosen by God as the 'Bab' (the gate). The claim caused fury in Iran which was eventually to lead to the Bab's execution by firing squad in July 1850.[11] One of his followers, Mirza Husayn Ali, known today as Baha'u'llah ('the glory of God'), claimed that he was the Madhi (Messiah) who had been promised by the Bab.

The Bab was a prolific writer, but there is no definite canon of Scripture in Bahai. The basic teachings of Bahai have been summed up in the dictum, 'The earth is but one country and mankind its citizens.' Bahaism is syncretistic, and claims to be the ultimate fulfilment of Judaism, Buddhism, Islam, Zoroastrianism, Hinduism and Christianity. While proclaiming the merits of all world religions, Bahaism also insists that these faiths must concede to the supremacy of the revelation of Baha'u'llah. Bahais believe that mankind is heading towards a world catastrophe out of which a golden age will emerge. Only the Bahais themselves will be prepared to rule the new world in which war shall cease and all people will live like brothers.

Hindu Tradition

It is from Hinduism and Buddhism that the majority of the new religious movements have emerged in the West. Gurus belonging to many Hindu traditions, both ancient and modern, brought their message to the West. These include the Hara Krishna Movement (ISKCON), Swami Sivanada's 'Divine Life Society', and Transcendental Meditation.

The International Society for Krishna Consciousness became for many people the symbol of the invasion of Asian religion into Western society in the 1970s. In 1965, at the age of seventy, a former pharmacist from Bengal sailed to New York. His name was A. C. Bhaktivedanta Swami Prabhupada. He went with a typically Hindu philosophy focused upon the Hindu god Krishna. Prabhupada taught that the lack of inner peace that people know is caused by *karma,* which locks the individual into an endless cycle of births and rebirths. By chanting the name of the god Krishna, it is possible to break out of the slow and painful cycle and return 'back to the godhead' (Krishna).

Transcendental Meditation has become the most successful of all the meditation groups. The movement was founded by Maharishi Mahesh Yogi in 1957. The bearded, white-robed yogi popularised his simplified Hindu meditation techniques under the initials TM. In 1982, Maharishi announced his world strategy to set up 3,600 centres, one for each million people of earth. Each of these centres would have one TM teacher per 1,000 people in the general population. It is claimed that as soon as 1% of the world's population practice TM the world will be saved from war and destruction.

Hara Krishna and TM were essentially Hindu imports slightly modified for the Western culture. Other cults have emerged from within Western society drawing much upon various elements of the Hindu worldview. This syncretism has spored many groups, and is well illustrated by Scientology.

Scientology was founded by L. Ron Hubbard, born in 1911 in Nebraska, USA. He first achieved success as a science fiction writer, but it was his book *Dianetics: The Modern Science of Mental Health* which brought him public recognition in 1950. Brooks Alexander writing of Hubbard says that he

> stripped away the gongs, incense, shaved heads and other cultur-
> ally alien trappings and replaced them with business suits, elec-
> tronic gadgetry and the jargon of self-improvement. At the same
> time, he retained the core values of the Eastern occult worldview.
> Hubbard made the first systematic attempt to unite the search for
> self with the search for ultimate reality and to present it in a West-
> ern technological package.[12]

Hubbard taught that all humans are 'thetans', by which he would mean uncreated gods who repeatedly reincarnate. 'Thetan' is approximately equivalent to what most Westerners would rec-ognise as the soul, or real self. It is immortal and non-physical, and came to inhabit a particular human body at the moment of conception. During the course of millions of years, and endless reincarnations, the thetans have forgotten their real existence. Hubbard claimed that through Scientology the negative forces, 'engrams', which have developed during these prior lives may be eradicated, and the person become aware of his full potential.

An individual undergoes Scientology auditing in order to rid himself of engrams implanted during previous lives. The E-meter was heralded as a major advance in the development of his therapy, but is in reality what most people know as a lie detector.[13] Through the process of counselling, an individual may become 'clear', by which is meant an 'operating thetan'. According to Scientology, 'clear' means calmness and serenity, and some adverts promise an IQ in excess of 135.

Reasons for growth of sects and cults

Why do people become part of a sect or cult? The answer is obviously complex. H. Richard Niebuhr proposed that sect-type movements emerged from economically deprived groups.

Although this has been criticised on several points, the deprivation model provides one of the most useful to understand the process. Glock said that the concept of deprivation, 'refers to any and all of the ways that an individual or group may be, or feel disadvantaged in comparison either to other individuals or groups or to an internalised set of standards.'[14] Several common factors may be identified.

1) A general dissatisfaction with their current worldview, and a quest for a holistic explanation of reality. The person wants an explanation of the world which will allow him to cope, not just physically, or spiritually, but totally. For various reasons the contemporary worldview fails to answer the felt-needs of the individual or community. All too often the existing religion fails even to appreciate the problem, never mind present an answer.

Even so, the new religion must be meaningful in terms of the indigenous worldview. If the movement grows up within the culture it tends to exemplify the issues as a matter of course. If, however, the movement is introduced from outside, it must make appropriate accommodations to the local culture. This will usually require reinterpretation or syncretism. This is well illustrated by the introduction of yoga into the West where it has been almost stripped of its Hindu context.

2) A desire for a new experience of the transcendent. From out of the everyday problems the person wants to be caught up with a sense of sublime rapture. It is often accompanied by intense pleasure, and in some cases simultaneously by pain. This is a mystical experience which is not easily explained, but readily appreciated by other members of the movement.

3) A quest for community in a world in which the individual is lost. This may be the reformulation of the traditional tribal community, or the formation of a new community from out of a fragmented individualistic society. This is illustrated with the Children of God which stressed the close inter-relationships of a family, leading eventually to sexual intimacy and perversion.

Frequently there is a process by which the person is initiated into the new community. They move from the status of being 'outsiders' to becoming 'insiders', and members of the 'believing community'. This usually occurs through a process of education (or as some would say, 'indoctrination') in the beliefs and history of the movement. The individual finally becomes committed to these views, and the community becomes a place in which the member feels at home. If, for any reason, the movement disintegrates, or the member feels it necessary to withdraw, the person always feels a deep sense of loss akin to bereavement.

4)   The authoritative revelation is often personified in the one to whom the initial revelation is given. This 'prophet' figure has opened a doorway to a new understanding of reality, and so requires a commitment and loyalty from his followers. With time, and especially after the prophet's death, a total mythology develops about the prophet's life. The prophet becomes an idealised figure, or even a god.

Max Weber appropriated the concept of charisma from theology, and applied it to the role of such a leader.[15] They exhibit a deep sense of call and mission as we have seen with Joseph Smith, Ghulam Ahmad, Siddartha Gautama, Sun Myung Moon and others. In order for the movement to grow, the leader must not only attract followers, he has also to develop an organisation. It is out of this dual requirement that many difficulties arise.

5)   People are seeking for clear lines of authority with strong leadership. Not all religious movements require the same level of commitment, but all make specific demands on what should be believed and how one should behave. A new belief system is presented which purports to answer the fundamental questions being asked by the enquirer.

The African Independent Churches are often criticised by Protestants as being free from restraint because they sometimes allow polygamy. However, a closer study shows that they have many fixed rules relating to other issues raised by their traditional culture. In African culture, menstrual blood is regarded as being polluting. Is it therefore acceptable for a woman to enter the holy ground of a church during her period?

Western missionaries gave no consideration to this matter, but many of the independent churches give a clear directive that it is wrong. Many other such taboos and restrictions are imposed upon their followers if they want to know the blessing of God.

6) New religious movements often provide patterns for a new life-style. The way one dresses, length of one's hair, type of food eaten are subject to the group norms, and commands of the leader.

One of the most interesting features of the movements of the 1960s and 1970s was that their recruits in the West came from middle-class youth. These young people were rebelling against their parents' life-style marked by affluence and materialism. They accepted Eastern dress as a mark of their rejection of the Western establishment, and moved to live in communes rather than nuclear family units.

7) A new set of religious rituals stimulates a sense of excitement as the individual participates in something different from the old way of living. Amongst the North American Indians, the 'Ghost Dance' led to this feeling of participation in a common transcendent experience. In yoga, it is the act of meditation with the discipline it requires which gives the student a sense of participating in a new way of life. The very fact that Western society has encouraged the acceptance of innovation and change means that people are willing, and in many cases eager, to adopt that which was formerly considered as being exotic and even socially unacceptable.

8) A new religious movement also requires a positive programme for winning converts if it is to continue to grow. This requires the mobilisation of its members, and the use of mass media for communication of its message.

By the mid-1970s the new religious movements in the West had begun to disappear along with the dream of a transformed society. The media was asking, 'Where have all the hippies gone?' The age of affluence was over, and unemployment was becoming a serious problem. Starvation amongst many millions of people in Africa suddenly made environmental issues of major importance practically and not just theoretically.

In the 1980s something new began to take its place, and this was a wide variety of social movements and ideas. Some of these had survived from the 1960s, and others have developed from the same non-Christian traditions. This religious creativity has travelled in all directions influencing most of Western society. It currently goes under the name of the 'New Age'.

Notes

1. Turner, Harold. 'A Global Phenomenon', in Brockway & Rajashekar, *New Religious Movements and the Churches* (WCC: Geneva, 1987) p 5.
2. Hummel, Reinhart. *ibid* p 19.
3. Niebuhr, H. Richard. *The Social Sources of Denominationalism* (Shoestring Press: Hamden, 1954).
4. Social Trends (HMSO: London, 1985) *Christianity Today* (May 7, 1976).
5. Howells, Rulon S. *The Mormon Story* (Bookcraft: Salt Lake City, 1961) p 21.
6. Martin, Walter R. *The Maze of Mormonism* (Zondervan: Grand Rapids, 1962) pp 41–62.
7. Tanner, Jerald & Sandra. 'Mormonism' in David J. Hesselgrave, *Dynamic Religious Movement* (Baker Book House: Grand Rapids, 1978) p 204.
8. Tanner, ibid. p 220.
9. Davis, Deborah. *The Children of God* (Marshalls: Basingstoke, 1984) p 204.
10. Inniger, Merlin W. 'The Ahmadiya Movement: Islamic Renewal?' in *Dynamic Religious Movements* (Baker Book House: Grand Rapids, 1978) p 161.
11. Miller, William. *What is the Baha'i Faith?* (Eerdmans: Grand Rapids, 1977) p 21.
12. Chandler, Russell. *The New Age* (Word Books: Milton Keynes, 1988) p 72.
13. Annett, Stephen. *The Many Ways of Being* (Abacus: London, 1976) p 135.
14. Nelson, Geoffrey K. *Cults, New Religions and Religious Creativity* (Routledge & Kegan Paul: London, 1987) p 86.
15. Weber, Max. *The Sociology of Religion* (Methuen: London, 1965).

11

FLIGHT FROM SECULARISM:
The New Age Movement

'New Age' is a term which has grasped the imagination of many people throughout the Western world, including Christians. It is essentially a syncretism of ideas coming from a wide variety of non-Christian religions mixed with modern theories of philosophy and psychology. Within the all embracing term of New Age is included a profusion of sects, and spiritual phenomena. One essential element characterises them all, a flight from the secular worldview. This has resulted in the exponents of the movement drawing upon a vast array of other-worldly beliefs and practices.

Historical development

As with all movements, it is necessary to understand the historical development of the New Age movement, and to identify the roots from which it has arisen. We shall see that with the New Age many of these founding elements have come from out of the failures of the secular worldview.

Theosophy

In nineteenth-century Europe and America, various spiritual movements occurred as were discussed in the previous chapter. One of these was Theosophy. It was this movement, perhaps more than any other, which was first responsible for the popularising of Eastern esoteric teaching in the West. The Theosophical Society was founded in New York in 1875 by Madame Helena Petrovna Blavatsky (1831–91), an eccentric Russian mystic.

Theosophists believe that all great religions and the teachings of the wise throughout history have a certain core of basic knowledge which is referred to as theosophy. The principle doctrines are closely connected with Hindu traditions. The universe is regarded as a unity based upon certain fundamental universal laws. Mankind is part of a general evolutionary process. While the forms in which life expresses itself are transient, the human spirit is eternal. Thus, when a person dies the individualised spirit continues, and the spirit will in time be reincarnated into a new body. The individual's resulting earthly conditions are determined according to the law of *karma*. However within this, individuals have the power to free themselves from all human limitations and to experience reality directly through the process of meditation.[1]

Nina Easton, writing in *The Los Angeles Times* magazine, said that Blavatsky could be called 'a godmother of the New Age movement'.[2] It was one of her successors, Alice Bailey (1880–1949) who is credited with having coined the phrase, 'New Age', which recurs throughout her writings. The Theosophical Society is well organised with members grouped into branches or lodges. They have their own publishing house, and their books and pamphlets have had a wide circulation throughout the world. The author knows of a Christo-pagan group in Ghana which uses the writings of the Theosophical Society in its meetings.

Science

New Age ideas have not only been stimulated by religion, but also by modern scientific discoveries. As we have previously mentioned, Newton's theory of gravity is based on an assumed force acting at a distance between all pairs of bodies. Einstein's theory of relativity uses a field theory to consider gravitation in which every entity produces a gravitational field that permeates all surrounding space, but at a lower force further from its source. Though there are no major differences to the Newtonian model over short distances it has some major repercussions.

Einstein showed that gravity has some major effects upon the basic measuring devices of physics such as clocks, rulers, and light rays. For example, a clock close to the sun will run more slowly than an identical clock far out in space. In the presence of a strong gravitational field the sum of the angles of a triangle will not equal 180 degrees. Space-time makes up a four-dimensional non-Euclidean continuum which is curved. Light rays will therefore not necessarily travel in straight lines, but will be deflected by the gravitational field along the curvature of the space-time continuum.

The theories of relativity provide answers to phenomenon such as black holes in outer space. Most properties of a black hole are not observable because the space-time continuum around it is so curved that not even light escapes. To an observer outside, matter falling into a black hole takes forever to reach the event horizon which may be regarded as the radius of the black hole. On the other hand, for an observer with the matter falling into the black hole, the time will be very short indeed.[3] If it was possible to enter into a black hole without destruction some scientific models propose the possibility of entering new universes.

Einstein showed that the inertial mass of a body, m, is related to the total energy in that body, E, by the equation $E=mc^2$, where c is the speed of light. Matter which was once regarded as being so real and tangible is now seen as some type of force-field. Matter may be compressed down in collapsing stars to such a degree that it becomes 100,000 times as dense as water. The very nuclei of the atoms are stripped of their electrons and rigidly packed together. What we are perceiving when we look at matter is no more than electron clouds about nuclei which are at relatively great distances from each other. How real, therefore, is the world about us?

Cognition

Another area in which tremendous changes have occurred has been in the area of the Behaviourial Sciences. The study of other cultures has shown that what were once considered primitive peoples have very developed ways of thinking and behaving. As people looked out from the stressful life of the urban world they grew in admiration of the seemingly idyllic world of tribal societies. Many looked at these societies thinking they may have something valuable to teach Western man. Could it be that the proud Western culture had its defects?

This led to the very important concept which is that our culture affects the way we perceive reality. Newtonian dynamics held that it was possible for a person to observe reality directly and fully. As was described in Chapter 1, this concept has been questioned. The perception of human beings is now believed to be limited by their senses and attention. The mind struggles to formulate models of what the person considers to be real. Edward Sapir proposed the theory of 'forced observation', by which he meant that language actually defines experience for us in forcing the person to describe it in certain ways.[4] For example, the English language has tenses, but Chinese does not. The English speaker is therefore accustomed, or 'forced', to specify whether an event occurred in the past, present or future. Sapir would therefore conclude that the English person is 'programmed' to a particular perspective of time. We do not make our worldview; our worldview shapes us, and our perspective of reality. As Adam Smith put it:

> The child says, oh look, Mommy, a purple cow, and the mother says, there is not such a thing as a purple cow, sweetheart, and so the kid stops reporting purple cows, and gradually as he gets older the visual messages processed by his brain are modified and translated in terms of Mommy's world until he can't remember seeing a purple cow. (The purple cows then walk around with impunity, unseen by anyone.)[5]

Psychology

Yet another element in the growth of New Age thinking is that of 'Transpersonal Psychology'. This concept was initially formulated by William James,[6] Carl Jung,[7] and Aldous Huxley. Carl Jung, commencing from a study of schizophrenics, went on to make a study of dreams. He found certain common metaphors which reoccurred in dreams of people from various cultures. Below the level of the 'little dreams' of the individual consciousness, he discovered sets of universal symbols he considered as resulting from a common collective consciousness. The universal symbols which he called 'archetypes' formed the basis of a common mythology.

Jung was trying to find an answer to the sense of lostness and alienation within modern man, and concluded that this resulted from a lack of mythology. Jung was much impressed by the Peublo Indians whom he visited whilst in the United States. They seemed to him to have a much closer relationship to the earth, and a mythology which gave them meaning as a people. Their myths were often expressed as rituals whose symbolism resulted in a power of its own. Jung often quoted an old Peublo man called Mountain Lake, 'The Americans are all crazy because they think with their heads rather than their hearts.'

Abraham Maslow reported peak experiences in which a person is in a moment of bliss, beyond time and space, and even beyond good and evil. These experiences of altered consciousness have led to important questions about the whole nature of man and reality. These questions have been united to the issues of cognition. If the mind is only able to detect certain sense data, and his culture limits his thinking processes, could it be that humans are only perceiving a certain portion of reality. Is man operating at a very low level of cosmic consciousness?

The contemporary studies in the human brain led transpersonal psychologists to assume that it was the left hemisphere of the brain which was dominant in Western man. This hemisphere was the one which was most logical and analytical. The right hemisphere was essentially neglected, and so Western man lacked in his intuition and mythical awareness. As Mark Cosgrove points out, transpersonal psychologists have therefore argued that people must be educated in an intuitive mode of thought. By having their consciousness altered, people may develop to their full potential as persons.[8]

Many leaders in the New Age movement are not unlearned

followers of some peculiar cult, but those who have studied the social sciences, and followed the latest scientific discoveries. One merely has to read a book by Marilyn Ferguson and journals such as *New Humanity* to realise this fact.[9] New Agers make great use of the vocabulary of the social sciences, and ideas such as 'paradigm shift', and 'worldview' are common. Modern scientific discoveries have raised many questions of the secular worldview which gave birth to modern science. But, as we saw in the third chapter, the secular worldview has been unable to give satisfactory answers. The New Age movement is an attempt to formulate a new and more satisfying worldview for today's generation.

Jung postulated that the collective unconsciousness represents a biological substratum which expresses itself as symbols, and these modern man has almost lost. Among the more important of these archetypes are the wise old man, the earth mother, the masculine and feminine aspects of men and women, and the divine child. Jung points people to look away from modern society for the real answers to life. He points to societies such as the Pueblo of North America, and the African people he visited on one of his trips. These people are closer to original man and it is with them that the archetypes are most clear. Thus, the New Age movement looks back to primal societies, or to ancient Eastern religions, or even to ancient cultic rituals.

New Age and the media

As mentioned in the previous chapter, the contemporary roots of the New Age movement can be found among the counter-culture groups which emerged in the 1960s. Materialistic affluence with opportunities for sensual freedom lead to the formation of the 'flower people'. Drugs provided a means for 'mind trips' beyond the limitations of space and time. The Beatles played a key role through their music. Not only did they bring Maharishi Mahesh Yogi to the knowledge of their many followers, but their musical productions, such as

Sergeant Pepper's Lonely Hearts Club Band, advocated a new holistic approach to the meaning of life. George Harrison wrote the song 'My sweet Lord', in praise of Krishna. Eastern mysticism had suddenly become popular amongst young people throughout the Western world.

The term 'New Age' seems to have become associated with the 'Age of Aquarius' through the title song of the 1960s musical *Hair*. Aquarius became the symbol of the initiation of a new age. Marilyn Ferguson, a leading exponent of the New Age, wrote what has become a manifesto of New Age philosophy and titled it *The Aquarian Conspiracy*. Explaining the choice of title, she writes, 'Conspire, in its literal sense, means "to breathe together". It is an intimate joining. To make clear the benevolent nature of this joining, I chose the word Aquarian. Although I am unacquainted with astrological lore, I was drawn to the symbolic power of the pervasive dream in our popular culture: that after a dark, violent age, the Piscean, we are entering a millennium of love and light – in the words of the popular song, "The Age of Aquarius", the time of the mind's true liberation.'[10]

Terms like 'enlightenment', and 'higher states of consciousness' became popular. Many young people travelled the 'Hippie' trail to Nepal and India in search of meaning. At the same time numerous Hindu yogi travelled to the West to expound their particular schools of meditation and yoga. Many young people associated themselves with their particular yogi in a search for mystic experience. Overnight it seemed that many knew a paradigm shift from the secular to the mystical.

The New Age has had a powerful influence upon the mass media, not only through the Beatles and Shirley MacLaine. New Age concepts have become commercially profitable especially when linked with science fiction and fantasy. Jungian psychologists would say that science fiction has in fact become the mythology of Western man. Here the archetypes identified by Jung are explored within cultural overlays of extra-terrestrial intelligence.

The *Star Wars* series of films provides an interesting

example. Luke Skywalker flies in to try and drop a bomb into a small duct which was the only vulnerable spot on the 'Death Star' (the massive enemy space-ship). Other heroes have failed to achieve the task even though they have used all their high technology, but Luke is called upon to use his intuition and not his computers. He (of course!) succeeds where all others have failed. 'The force' was with him!

Star Wars, *The Empire Strikes Back*, and *The Dark Crystal* have all been major box office successes. Television too has known the influence of this way of thinking with even children's cartoons like *He-man* and *The Masters of the Universe* manifesting a mythical dimension. *Dungeons and Dragons* has come to be one of the best selling, and most commercially profitable games. It must be noted that many of these films and games are produced not to propagate New Age ideas, but because they present themes which are desired within Western society, and therefore are successful business ventures.

Within the broader culture there are numerous other influences of New Age thought. Major corporations have sought to increase the performance of their managers and workers through meditation techniques. Holistic health food has become commercially big business. Most leisure centres offer courses on yoga as a normal part of their health programme.

Before we can try to discuss the themes which characterise the New Age worldview, it is necessary first to try and identify the various streams within this complex movement.

Streams within the New Age movement

To apply an analytical approach to studying the New Age movement in a sense typifies a Western analytical approach. The New Age movement would reject such a rational approach preferring synthesis rather than analysis. However, an analytical approach allows one to arrive at an objective understanding of what is currently happening in this complex movement.

The first stream consists of those who look for their inspiration to living religions of the East. Hinduism, Buddhism, and

Taoism are the most common. These religions, as we have seen in previous chapters, place great stress upon the mystic experience. However, other religions also have a mystical dimension. Islam has Sufism, Judaism has Kabbalah, and even Christianity has had its mystics. These have provided additional channels for practice by New Age exponents.

The second stream looks back beyond the coming of Christianity to countries now dominated by European peoples. In Europe, the exploration of pre-Christian celtic and Saxon religion is growing in popularity along with witchcraft which is assumed to be a pre-Christian religion. In America, the shamanistic practices of the North American Indian healers have received renewed interest since 1985.

A third stream has turned to various forms of occultic magic. Spiritism has been revived in a new psychological form under the name of 'channelling'. Ancient methods of divination are currently being used such as the rune stones from ancient Viking origin, now on sale in a modern commercially packaged form from your High Street newsagent. Ouija boards, tarot cards, books of horoscopes, and astrology are widely used.

Figure 11.1 is an attempt to show the major streams diagrammatically. In this chapter we will concentrate upon that aspect of the movement deriving its inspiration from Eastern mystical practices. It is essential to realise that this movement is in a constant state of flux, and new aspects are developing.

New Age worldview themes

It need hardly be said that any attempt to analyse such a complex and diverse movement is liable to be an over-simplification of the truth. However, such an analysis can help to identify many common fundamental themes which, as would be expected, are similar to those of the Hindu worldview discussed in the fifth chapter. Norman Geisler listed fourteen doctrines which are typical of New Age religions, and these have been incorporated in this analysis.[11]

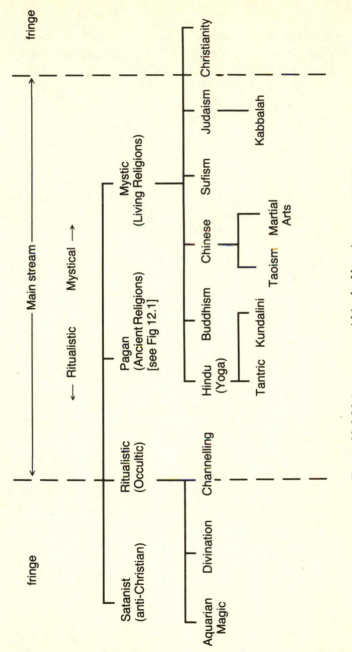

Figure 11.1 Major streams within the New Age movement

The Cosmos

The cosmos is conceived as being pure, undifferentiated, universal energy, or 'life force'. Everything is one vast, interconnected process which may be considered as deity. In other words, God is all and all is God. God is an impersonal force. This is essentially the pantheism characteristic of the Hindu worldview. This assumption leads to many of the same themes as found within traditional Hinduism, but as we shall see there are some important differences.

> All true mystics have agreed that the essence of life is soul, or consciousness. That all living creatures, whether, plants, bacteria, dinosaurs, shellfish, animals, birds or men are, in essence, drops in the Divine Ocean of Being, Consciousness or Life. The material universe too, is His creation, His play or projection, and there is no part in which He is not present. He is within everything, there is nothing in which He is not the inward and continuously active Creator. He is within everything, and yet he is also all of all.[12]

First, the material world is regarded as no more than a projection of deity, and its appearance of being a distinct reality is only an illusion. The argument for this does not come from the religious concepts of Hinduism, but the discoveries of modern science. Atoms were once thought of as the basic building blocks of the physical world, but now they are conceived of as energy fields – a fold in the space-time continuum. As the New Age scientist, Dr Rupert Sheldrake writes: 'Karl Popper once said that through modern physics materialism has transcended itself, because matter is no longer the basic reality. Matter is now thought of as energy bound within fields. Fields don't arise from matter, matter arises from fields. Fields are more fundamental than matter.'[13]

Second, the undefinable reality which transcends all else may be perceived in a multitude of forms which are expressed in the major world religions. All religions are assumed to be essentially one. Jesus, Buddha, Muhammad and Lao-tse all essentially taught the same thing which was how one could become united with the One. Thus, New Age exponents are surprisingly tolerant of all religions, and are willing for a syncretism of any. Some have therefore sought to return to the tribal religions characteristic of ancient peoples before the coming of Christianity. This will be discussed in the next chapter as the neo-pagan dimension to the New Age movement. Others have turned to the Hindu, Buddhist, or Taoist religions.

Thirdly, reality is a total, all embracing whole and there is no distinction between natural and supernatural. Dreams and fantasies are of equal reality to objective experiences. Nature itself is regarded as a reflection of ultimate reality, and so the environment must be cared for and preserved. Ecology, and so-called green issues, therefore become important on the New Age agenda. The Findhorn community, for example, was founded in 1962 beside the Moray Firth in the Northeast of Scotland and publishes a magazine called *One Earth*. The magazine claims that the community has 'become famous for "growing very large vegetables on sand dunes by talking to the nature spirits", and entertaining the notion that all life is one .... We know that everything is alive and interdependent. We are all essential crew on Spaceship Earth.'[14]

The Self

Developing out of the premise that all is one, humanity is therefore one. People are part of the divine because the whole cosmos is God. 'I am God,' shouts Shirley MacLaine.

According to New Age thinking, man is basically a spiritual being, not a material one. Humans like everything else are only extensions of the Oneness and individuality is only part of the illusion. Humanity is not made up of many individual selves, there is but One Self. A person's main task is therefore to discover the reality that he or she is divine. This is not achieved through objective, but subjective experiences which occur within the mind.

What is the mind? Is the mind the same as the brain? Where do bright ideas, emotions or dreams come from? The human brain is far more complex than can be studied by modern science. There are as many as 100 billion nerve cells in the human brain. Science has known for some time that different parts of the brain serve different functions. The left hemisphere, for example, does the thinking whilst the right does the feeling. The left hemisphere controls speech, compartmentalises, organises, and analyses. The right hemisphere is more musical and sexual than the left thinking in images, and detecting whole patterns. New Age would argue that Western man has allowed the left hemisphere to dominate and sabotage our full potential as humans. We need to still the chatter of the left hemisphere and become aware of the messages from the more mystical half. The utilisation of the two hemispheres creates something new which is far more than the sum of the parts, and different from either.

Reincarnation is another common concept of the New Age. This is the Hindu notion that the soul progresses through many life cycles according to the working out of one's *karma*. The final aim is the merging with the absolute One. The escape from this endless cycle is only achieved through mystical knowledge which is the key to being awakened from our ignorance of divinity.

Pain and human illness are considered to derive from an imbalance of spiritual energy. In the Chinese worldview this was called *chi*, and in Hindu *prana*. Healing therefore requires a balancing of these various forces within the body. This may be achieved through yoga, acupuncture, natural herbs (vegetarianism is common), and even psychic surgery. Holistic medicine is one of the most expanding and influential aspects of the New Age movement. It carries with it a totally different concept of the nature of sickness and healing than that of established Western secular concepts of health.

Secular medicine	Holistic medicine
Body seen as a machine.	Body seen as a dynamic system.
Body and mind separate.	Holistic perspective.

Mind is secondary to organic illness.	Mind primary or co-equal in all illnesses.
Emphasis upon eliminating symptoms, disease.	Emphasis upon achieving maximum of being well.
Reliance upon qualitative information and tests.	Reliance upon intuition and subjective reports.

This comparison contrasts just a few of the major differences which are listed by others.[15]

Community

The emphasis upon the individual's liberation from *karma* through enlightenment tends to place the emphasis upon the individual. It is for the individual to achieve cosmic consciousness through their own personal quest. Thus, although the aim is to achieve unity with the One, it is achieved through individualistic means. Terms such has 'self-actualisation', 'human potential' and 'self-potential' have become part of the New Age vocabulary.

Within Hinduism the effect of *karma* leads to the caste system. Here the caste into which a person is born is a result of *karma* resulting from previous lives. This is one aspect of Hindu philosophy which has not been brought into New Age thinking. On the contrary, New Age has placed the emphasis upon the equality of all, and it has especially sought to balance the disparity between men and women.

The emphasis upon unity leads to the need for world peace which therefore becomes an important theme within the New Age movement. Political boundaries are becoming obsolete, and one government body should rule the world. Marxism and capitalism are regarded as two complementary political systems which are both failing and need to be united.

What is needed now is for an explicit recognition that Marxism v Capitalism is not a 'holy war' as some crusaders of dogma would have it but is an example of a complementarity. Marxist and Capitalist socio-economies are complementary concepts, neither one is wrong or better than the other and that both perspectives are needed to fully understand a social system that works without detrimental effects on groups or individuals.[16]

Time

Hinduism perceives of time as being an endless cycle of coming into being and then decay. Time is cyclic. This is seen both in the individual perspective as with reincarnation, but also within the universal periods of history. The universal periods of time are revealed through astrological epochs. The movement from the period of Pisces to that of Aquarius is therefore seen to be of major importance. There is some discrepancy regarding the date at which we enter the age of Aquarius. Most involved with the New Age say we entered the 'New Age' in 1983, but others prefer to say we will enter in the year 2000.

The concept of time held by the New Age movement is different from that of the secular worldview with its strict linearity and universality. New Age accepts differences in the flow of time which are encountered during meditation and out-of-body experiences. This is commonly what is perceived by individuals when on some occasions time appears to pass quickly whilst on other occasions it appears to drag. This is linked with the Einsteinian concept of time being affected by inertia and velocity.

Value

As with the Hindu worldview, the thesis of monism leads to the assumption that there are no absolutes. All is relative! There is no such thing as an absolute dichotomy between good and evil. Good and evil are what particular societies label them. People are essentially good although they may do bad things.

The only sin within the New Age would appear to be ignorance of unity and belief in an individual self. If All is One, then, unless violence is used, no form of sexual activity violates another person's sanctity. Rajneesh, like many New Age gurus, has removed sexual limits as inhibitive of building deep social relations. Sensuous pleasure is encouraged, and yet the ultimate teaching is that the material universe is merely an illusion. Most Hindu gurus would turn away from such worldly indulgences, and seek to deny bodily pleasures in their desire for reality.

Christian reaction to the New Age movement

It was in 1983 that Constance E. Cumbey, a semi-retired lawyer from Detroit, shocked the evangelical community in the States. Her book *Hidden Dangers of the Rainbow* contended that the New Age movement is a sinister conspiracy led by Satan to take over the world.[17] In so doing, both Christians and Jews would be eliminated, and the universal worship of the Antichrist established. This so-called conspiracy theory has been further developed by Texe Marrs, a retired US Air Force officer, in his books, *Dark Secrets of the New Age*,[18] and *Mysterious Mark of the New Age*.[19]

These, and other similar writers, have sought to link Bible prophecy, particularly Daniel and Revelation, to New Age objectives. Their books have sold well, and have caused many Christians to be alerted to the reality of the New Age movement. However, their expositions have resulted in an almost fanatical exposure of any seeming New Age influences. Two important questions arise for the Christian. The first relates to whether there is a New Age conspiracy, and the second to how the New Age is affecting the church.

First, is there such a thing as a New Age conspiracy? Marilyn Ferguson, a leading New Ager, wrote her book entitled *The Aquarian Conspiracy* in 1980. She claims that there is a conspiracy, but it is 'a conspiracy without political doctrine. Without a manifesto. With conspirators who seek power only to disperse it, and whose strategies are pragmatic, even scientific, but whose perspective sounds so mystical that they hesitate to discuss it.'[20] The collusion she claims is one of shared assumptions rather than centralised planning.

Russell Chandler argues that it seems inconsistent to assume that such an unstructured, effervescent collection of movements and ideas which are embraced by the term 'New Age' could be part of some gigantic, centralised conspiracy against the church headed by Satan.[21] A more moderate view is that expressed by Douglas Groothuis in *Unmasking the New Age* where he writes: 'The New Age movement is better viewed as a worldview shift than a unified global conspiracy. This is not to minimise its influence but to recognise it as an intellectual, spiritual and cultural force to be reckoned with in all sobriety.'[22]

I would personally agree with both Chandler and Groothuis and consider the New Age movement a paradigm shift resulting from a synthesis of themes. As we have seen in a study of the Hindu worldview, many of its themes have been adopted into what has been called the New Age movement. During this process there has been a syncretisation of the themes with those of the secular worldview. Some Hindu themes have been accepted almost in total, whilst some secular themes have been only slightly modified.

For example, yoga is a well known Hindu religious activity in India to aid meditation and release (*moksah*). However, no one in India would associate yoga with physical exercise as it is so often portrayed in the West. In India, yoga is regarded as worship. Similarly, the law of *karma* is accepted by many in the New Age movement, but the Indian concept of caste has not been adopted. Caste is an anathema to Westerners, and so has been filtered out in the process of Westernisation of Eastern religions. What we see with the New Age movement is the evolution of a new worldview based upon a syncretisation of Eastern and primal worldviews with the secular.

The second question which needs to be addressed by Christians is regarding the influence of New Age thinking within the church. A few groups are seeking to reconcile Christianity with New Age thinking. One such group is the Omega Order headed by Canon Peter Spink, now licensed by the Bishop of Bath and Wells to function as an Anglican priest in these dioceses. Canon Spink has said: 'We find many come to us because they want to relate to Christianity, but they want to find in Christianity the possibility of interpretive awareness that they have known in the East.'[23] He goes on to say: 'In the Church there is a steadily higher level of inquiry especially among the young clergy, and it is important to show the complete integration of historical Christianity with the New Age Movement.... There is a shift from outer devotionalism to interior awareness.'[24] Those holding to such a view tend to speak of 'Christ Consciousness', and see salvation as being the refusal to allow the least concession to, or belief in evil.

Other church leaders have been denounced by some Christians who consider that they have unwittingly been making use of New Age thinking. Roy Livesey warns of the dangers of New Age teaching within the church.[25] He lists five major areas where he claims there has been a distortion of biblical truth.

1) Positive confession: This would include such areas as prosperity teaching, and the views of some that one should claim health or wealth, by faith in Christ.

2) Self-esteem: Robert Schuller[26] has been criticised for his use of the terms 'Possibility Thinking' and 'self-esteem'.[27] Schuller has had a very influential ministry in the US, and has made use of psychological ideas of thinking positively.

3) Inner healing: Generally regarded as the ministry of healing of past memories and damaged emotions.

4) 'Signs and Wonders': The ministry of healing often including the gift of words of knowledge, laying on of hands, and 'fainting in the Spirit'.

5) Holistic medicine: The use of homeopathic medicine is especially noted.[28]

However, just because some aspects of Christian teaching show a parallel with New Age concepts, they should not be immediately labelled as such. There is a great danger in drawing guilt-by-association especially when words such as 'holistic', 'human potential', 'networking', 'paradigm', 'rainbow', 'self-realisation', and 'Spaceship Earth' are considered New Age. The rainbow is a beautiful biblical symbol of God's promise to mankind. Why should this symbol be labelled as New Age and handed over to that movement? Christians relating meaningfully to the world at the end of the twentieth century need to address the same sort of issues as faced by the New Age movement.

As with all new religious movements, they develop around questions which have failed to be answered by the existing worldview. As we saw in the third chapter, the secular worldview has failed to provide an answer to the meaning for an individual's personal existence. The question, 'Why am I here?' goes unanswered. The New Age provides an answer in cosmic consciousness. It also has the advantage of the excitement of any novelty in that it is new and not merely a return to established patterns. What is the Christian answer to these questions?

The global ecological problems find some sort of answer within the New Age philosophy. A unity within the total cosmos leads to a concern for planet earth. A worldview concerned with the earth produces an awareness of ecological issues almost in a chicken and egg relationship. Christians likewise should have a clearly biblical ecology.

Discernment is needed, but Christians should avoid the danger of seeing 'New Age' under every proverbial bed. At a time when many people are fleeing from the secular worldview, the church needs to ask why few are turning to Christianity. The church has for too long been under the influence of secularism, and it is necessary for it now to be a living witness to the biblical revelation.

Notes

1. Annett, Stephen. *The Many Ways of Being* (Abacus: London, 1976) pp 110–112.
2. Chandler, Russell. *Understanding the New Age* (Word Books: Milton Keynes, 1988) p 47.
3. *Encyclopaedia Britannica* (Encyclopaedia Britannica, Inc: Chicago, 1981), Micropedia Vol 2, p 61.
4. Sapir, Edward. *Culture, Language, and Personality* (University of California Press: Berkeley, 1958) 398.4.
5. Cosgrove, Mark P. *Psychology Gone Awry* (IVP: Leicester, 1979) p 84.
6. James, William. *Varieties of Religious Experience* (Longmans, Green & Co: London, 1902).
7. Jung, Carl. 'Synchronicity: An Acasual Connecting Principle', in

Ornstein, Robert E., ed. *The Nature of Human Consciousness* (Freeman: San Francisco, 1973) pp 445–457.

8. Cosgrove, Mark P., *op cit*, pp 84–100.
9. Ferguson, Marilyn. *The Aquarian Conspiracy* (Paladin Grafton Books: London, 1988).
10. Ferguson, *ibid*, p 19.
11. Geisler, Norman L. 'The New Age Movement', *Evangelical Review of Theology*, Vol 11, No 4, October 1987, p 307.
12. Davidson, John. 'The Golden Womb and the Formative Mind', in *New Humanity*, April-May 1989, p 10.
13. Sheldrake, Rupert. 'Habits of Nature', *One Earth*, Vol 8 Autumn 1988, p 30.
14. *One Earth*, Vol 8 issue 3 Autumn 1988, p 2.
15. Ferguson, *op cit*, pp 270–1.
16. Churcher, Peter R. 'Complementarity: a Philosophy without Division', in *New Humanity*, August-September, 1989, pp 5–6.
17. Cumbey, Constance E. *Hidden Dangers of the Rainbow* (Huntingdon House: Shreveport, 1983).
18. Maars, Texe. *Dark Secrets of the New Age* (Crossway Books: Westchester, 1987).
19. Maars, Texe. *Mystery Mark of the New Age* (Crossway Books: Westchester, 1988).
20. Ferguson, *op cit*, p 23.
21. Chandler, Russell. *Understanding the New Age* (Word Books: Milton Keynes, 1988) pp 225–234.
22. Groothuis, Douglas. *Unmasking the New Age* (IVP: Downers Grove, 1986) p 35.
23. Spink, Peter. 'In Pursuit of Self-awareness', in *Omega News* Autumn 1989, p 5.
24. Quanjer, Johan. 'A Visit to the Omega Order', *The New Humanity* April-May 1989, Year 15, No. 86, p 15.
25. Livesey, Roy. *Understanding Deception: New Age Teaching in the Church* (New Wine Press: Chichester, 1987).
26. Lawhead, Alice and Stephen. *Pilgrim's Guide to the New Age* (Lion Publishing: Tring, 1986) p 28.
27. Schuller, Robert. *Your Church has a fantastic Future! A Possibility Thinker's Guide to a Successful Church* (Regal Books: Ventura, 1986).
28. Livesey, Roy. *Understanding Alternative Medicine* (New Wine Press: Chichester, 1985).

12

THE OLD RELIGION IN THE NEW AGE:
Neo-paganism

One of the most surprising movements of recent times has been the growth of paganism and witchcraft within Western societies. Many thousands of people both in North America and Europe are now calling themselves 'pagans' or 'neo-pagans'. In general, these people consider themselves part of the New Age movement, but for their inspiration they look to those religions that antedate Christianity and monotheism. They, therefore, embrace a whole series of beliefs and practices drawing inspiration from Norse, Greek, Roman, Celtic, and Egyptian religions together with the surviving primal religions of the world.

Re-emergence of primal beliefs in the West

At one time people would never apply to themselves terms such as 'pagan' and 'witch', because they were regarded as inferior and uncivilised. The word 'pagan' actually comes from the Latin 'paganus' which means a country dweller, and is itself derived from 'pagus', the Latin word for village. By the end of the fourth century the word pagan became a derogatory term in Rome used of the uncivilised. Today, people are willing to apply these terms to themselves even publicly.

Why have these beliefs re-emerged within Christianised secular culture? When many primal societies are converting from these beliefs, why are some people now beginning to accept them? Where did neo-pagan religion come from? The anthropologist Linda Jencson has come to conclusions similar to my own research, and has expressed them consisely in the sub-title of her article, 'Anthropology as midwife to a new religion.'[1] Research by anthropologists into traditional religions and folklore during the last century have served to spread those very practices amongst their own informants, and by their writing, to new generations.

Witchcraft

Witchcraft and ritual magic was first given a pseudo-scientific standing through the theories of the anthropologist Margaret Murray in her book *The Witch Cult in Western Europe*.[2] Her views were expressed in a more popular way in the article she wrote on 'Witchcraft' in the fourteenth edition of *Encyclopaedia Britannica* (1929).[3] Murray put forward the theory that the witches of Western Europe were the lingering adherents of a once general pagan religion that has been displaced, though not completely, by Christianity. Margaret Murray was a recognised anthropologist and Egyptologist, but her views provoked a storm of controversy. Many of her critics pointed out that there is no record of covens as such prior to the fifteenth century, and they criticised her sources as being unreliable. She died in 1963, at the age of one hundred years, but admitted before death that she was a witch herself.[4]

Margaret Murray found an eager follower in the person of Gerald B. Gardner (1884–1964) who has been called everything from the 'Grand Old Man of Witchcraft' by his followers to a 'dirty old man' by his detractors. Gardner was born into a well-to-do family in the north of England in 1884. In his early years he suffered from asthma which provided the excuse for his Irish nurse called 'Com' to take him abroad for winter months. This was actually a way by which Com was able to have sexual relations with young men.[5] Com finally married and settled down in Ceylon, and it was arranged that Gardner should travel there and work on a tea plantation. He was a withdrawn young man and spent much of his time with the natives studying their beliefs and rituals. In 1908 he moved to Borneo where he came to know the Dyaks, a people who had formerly been head-hunters.

He returned to England in 1936, and continued to pursue his interest in folk religion. In 1955 he wrote the book *Witchcraft Today* in which he claimed to have discovered centuries-old covens, still practising their ancient 'craft' in modern Britain. Murray wrote the preface for the book in which she writes:

> Dr Gardner has shown in his book how much of the so-called 'witchcraft' is descended from ancient rituals, and has nothing to do with spell-casting and other evil practices, but is the sincere expression of the feelings toward God which is expressed, perhaps more decorously though not more sincerely, by modern Christianity in church services. But the processional dances of the drunken Bacchantes, the wild prancings round the Holy Sepulchre as recorded by Maundrell at the end of the seventeenth century, the jumping dance of the medieval 'witches', the solemn zikr of the Egyptian peasant, the whirling of the dancing dervishes, all have their origin in the desire to be 'Nearer, my God, to Thee', and to show by their actions that intense gratitude which the worshippers find themselves incapable of expressing in words.[6]

In later years Gardner founded and was curator to the Museum of Witchcraft and Magic on the Isle of Man. It was, however, his ability of catching the attention of the news media which catalysed the growth of neo-paganism. To Gardner, witchcraft was a nature religion in which the witches met in covens led by a priestess. They worshipped two principal deities, the god of forests and what lies beyond, and the great Triple goddess of fertility and rebirth. The participants met in the nude in a nine-foot circle and raised power from their bodies through dancing and meditation.

Gardner's writing and the opening of the witchcraft museum led to a flood of people wanting to be initiated into covens. Gardner and his associates duly obliged, and witchcraft's renaissance had begun. Today some followers of Gardner would themselves question whether Gardner had discovered an ancient coven, or had made the whole thing up.[7] Even so, the movement came at a responsive time and has grown in many quarters. The 1970s and 1980s have seen massive growth of books and articles written by witches on various aspects of 'The Craft'.

The Celtic Tradition

Following the 'flower people' of the 1960s, numerous tight-knit groups emerged based around Eastern gurus. These include many of the sects referred to in the previous chapter. However, the style changed in the 1980s, and the creativity allowed by neo-paganism became a major attraction for many. In Europe, the neo-pagan movement became an attempt to rediscover ancient Celtic traditions, and so such groups will label themselves as Irish, Scots, or Welsh traditions. *Inner Keltia* is a leading Scottish journal devoted to 're-animating virtually every aspect of Keltic-Pagan culture and spirituality'.[8]

This has led to an increasing interest in ancient Celtic religion and culture. Many of the ancient Celtic legends are written and discussed in the magazines of the Celtic movement.

> Angus Og, his name means the 'everyoung' Lord of Tir-Nan-Ouge the land of youth, is perhaps one of the most ancient Deities in Eire and Alba...we can see his origins as a Horned Deity and his evolution to the Gaelic God of Youth and Love. For the Shamans among you he may appear to you as a white Swan with a golden chain around its neck, as for the Magicians his physical help may be sought by shaking an Ash Tree at dawn. For the singles it is said a prayer to Angus will reveal your true love in your dreams to you.[9]

Northern Tradition

Others have turned to Norse paganism which is often referred to as the 'northern tradition'. Britain, it is claimed, is a land with two ancient traditions, the Celtic and the Germanic (Northern).[10] They have therefore turned to a study of Scandinavian myths and legends. They may call themselves 'Odinists', or 'Asatru' which in the old Norse language means the belief in the gods. There is a general assumption that the Norse religion is connected with Nazis because the Nazis used the old Norse symbol. Rune lore, with the rune stones used for divination.

Shamanist

Margot Adler regards the neo-pagan movement in the US, as being, in part, a search by up-rooted Europeans to find their roots as ancient peoples.[11] Some have looked back to Europe, and others have turned to the ancient religions of North America and especially the anthropologically well documented beliefs in 'Shamanism'.

Carlos Castaneda and Professor Michael Harner did much to popularise shamanism in the 1980s.[12] Harner is a noted anthropologist who has been visiting professor at Colombia and Yale Universities. He has made considerable studies of the Sioux and Jivaro Indian shaman, and has claimed to have experienced the initiatory visions of a shaman. Linda Jencson writes: 'My witch-teacher modified Harner's Central American shamanistic teachings only slightly to fit her Wiccan worldview.'[13] Harner's shamanistic workshops have been a considerable source of stimulus to the neo-pagan movement in the States. His drumming tapes to accompany shamanic trance journeys are now available commercially.

Mediterranean Tradition

The religious creativity found within neo-paganism is drawn from a multitude of ancient traditions. The Fellowship of Isis has its temple at Clonegal Castle, Eire, and draws upon ancient Egyptian religious sources. They claim to have members in 62 countries, with some 4,000 in Nigeria.[14] Gnosticism, a religion which was a major problem to Christianity in the fifth century, is another stream of inspiration for the pagan movement.

Others have reacted from the Christian tradition as a counter-culture movement, and have adopted Satan as their deity. Neo-pagans would not regard satanists as part of their movement, because satanists look to the Christian tradition for their rituals whilst neo-pagans return to the ancient pre-Christian traditions for their inspiration.

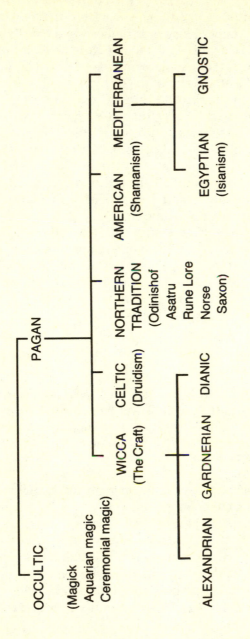

Figure 12.1 Major streams in the paganist movement

In the popular press, the term 'witch' has often been used to cover all these groups. This tends to merely add to the confusion in understanding this movement. Figure 12.1 is an attempt to identify some of the main streams who derive their inspiration from pre-Christian religions. The terms witch, witchcraft, and wicca derive from the Old English 'wicca' which has to do with religion and magic. This stream has a number of overlapping traditions. The Gardnerians follow the rituals described by Gardner mentioned earlier. The Alexandrian tradition came out of a coven started by Alex Sanders in England. Alex claims to have been initiated by his grandmother in 1933. Dianic tradition stems from the ideas of Margaret Murray that witchcraft was an ancient Dianic cult.

The failure of the secular worldview to provide an answer to the reality and meaning of the inner feelings and emotions has led people to explore the pagan alternative which was once rejected by their ancestors. In so doing modern paganists are adapting primal beliefs to fashion what they would regard as a more meaningful worldview.

Neo-pagan worldview

> Paganism is not a dogmatic faith. We have no 'holy books', prophets or saviours. There is no One True Way with Paganism – rather a great diversity of approach to the faith, and a great variety of creative ways in which it finds expression, naturally arising from the infinite diversity of life.[15]

While neo-pagans would disagree on many things, it is possible to identify certain common features.

The first, and one of the most important principles, is that of polytheism. This must be understood as meaning more than the assumption that divinity is numerically multiple. Neo-pagans speak of reality – both divine and otherwise – as being multiple and diverse. Neo-pagans would reject the evolutionary theory of religions popularised in the last century in which societies developed from polytheism to monotheism. They do so because this leads to an inferior view of polytheism as opposed to monotheism.

The neo-pagan view is essentially pantheistic in which all nature is divinity and yet manifests itself in a profusion of forms. Thus gods and goddesses are connected with particular places, people and phenomena.

Secondly, if all of reality is actually divinity, then the world is holy and human beings are holy. Some neo-pagans would speak of a divinity immanent in all nature. The earth is seen as possessing a life of its own, and therefore requiring a profound reverence. This devotion is given to the Earth Mother goddess who may be called Gaia, Freyja, The Lady or some other title. The Earth Mother goddess is often worshipped in the three-fold form of maiden, mother and old crone.

This concern for the earth has also led to a common concern with ecology. Nigel Pennick writes:

> The Northern Tradition teaches that despite hundreds of years of physical abuse, Nature is not spiritually dead, but that spirituality is inherent in Nature. Nature is alive and hallowed by the imma-nent presence of the gods. People and gods are within Nature, and must work in partnership with the natural cycles or face the consequences.[16]

As an extension of this, all aspects of the natural world should be revered, as should places of power within it. Sacred places on the landscape cannot be understood by materialistic analysis, but must be appreciated as places of spiritual power. These places of power are considered to be joined together by ancient ley-lines. 'A basic definition of a ley is straightforward enough: leys are alignments of ancient sites stretching across the landscape.'[17] However, this simple definition is used to raise questions about the nature of the relationship between humans and the land, and an assumption that ancient people had a different perception of the environment than we do today.

Bruce Chatwin in his controversial book, *Songlines*, describes the labyrinth of invisible pathways which are claimed to meander all over Australia.[18] The theme which runs through the book is that deep in man's psyche is an affinity to nomadic life which for so long characterised human existence and has now been left behind. This has resulted in the restlessness within the human soul.[19]

For this reason many neo-pagans are involved with the Green movement, and certain ecology groups are even exploring pagan ideas.[20] Many of the women who protested at Greenham Common have neo-pagan sympathies. One of the most established pagan magazines is called *The Pipes of P.A.N.*, where P.A.N. stands for 'Pagans Against Nukes', and is 'an activist organisation dedicated to the banishment of nuclear technology from Earth, and the re-establishment of a culture that lives in harmony with her. We urge all pagans, of whatever land and tradition, to engage in political and magical work to achieve this end, that the Earth be Greened Anew.'[21]

Thirdly, the feminine nature of reality is stressed to counter the long held emphasis upon masculinity. The great mother goddess is a central concept of neo-paganism, although the male horned god is recognised. Dr Leo Martello, an initiated witch writes, '"In the beginning God made man," the Bible says. And of course Eve was fashioned out of Adam's rib! Witches and pagans today are apt to paraphrase the Biblical version into "In the beginning Goddess made woman.".'[22] In many branches of neo-paganism, the goddess is superior to the male god, whilst in others they are equal. Many claim that in paganism there is a religion in which women are not oppressed by men. Some female paganists have argued that all major world religions legitimate patriarchy because 'If god is male, then the male is god.' They view men as brutalising women through sexual violence and pornography, and dominating them through a stern, overbearing, male 'sky-god'.

The Women's Liberation movement of the 1970s has found powerful feminine symbols within neo-paganism. In societies that have traditionally oppressed women, it is claimed, there are few positive images of female power. Some of the most potent are witches. In these, one can sense the release of 'female energy'. Women, and men too, it is claimed, need to understand their own creative strength and divine nature by embracing the creative feminine of the goddess within.

The fourth common feature is the manipulation of the world by means of rituals. Candles, swords, cups, rods, and orbs are all part of the craft of modern paganism. Some groups draw upon the imagined traditions of the ancient Druids by practising their rituals at Stonehenge. Others retire to the seclusion of the countryside, and perform their rituals under the cloak of darkness. Neo-paganists recognise that much of what they practise is based upon mere conjecture of ancient practices, but they would claim that by innovation within these rituals, a person comes to a deeper experience of power as they come in tune with the earth. These discoveries are preserved by the group and practised with greater zeal.

One ritual that has been described is one of 'self blessing' which should be performed during the new moon. For the ritual one requires: salt, wine, water, and a candle. 'When you are ready to begin, sprinkle the salt on the floor and stand on it, lighting the candle. Let the warmth of the candle be absorbed into the body. Mix the water into the wine, meditating upon your reasons for performing the self blessing.'[23] Certain words are then uttered which it is claimed brings a sense of peace and calm. The ritual is best performed 'sky-clad' (nude).

Most rituals are performed as a group, and this requires the formation of a coven. A traditional coven in Wicca would number twelve working in a circle nine feet in diameter. The circle is regarded as sacred ground, a place between the worlds where contact with the gods becomes possible. Covens may make use of chanting or meditation to raise psychic energy within the circle. Many covens have a ritual for drawing down the goddess, symbolised by the moon, into a priestess who may go into a trance, or become possessed.

The popular press often makes reference to the 'Great Rite'. In this ritual the woman who has become possessed by the 'goddess' through the rite, and a man who has become possessed by the 'god' have sexual union. This form of ritual has been common amongst many primal societies, and it is noted in the Old Testament as being the central practice carried out in the 'high places' (1 Kings 14:23,24).

A fifth characteristic which is of growing importance is the 'out-of-body' experience which is especially seen in shamanistic groups. In one of Michael Harner's workshops, he would have the participants to lay on the floor in such a way that the small group form the shape of a 'spirit-canoe'. Each person is encouraged to visualise themselves riding in it down to the lower world. As Harner beats the drum, the participants chant the old Jivaro Indian chant: 'I have a spirit, spirit have I....'

Here is a transcript of one person's notes of a particular shamanistic journey:

> I enter the fireplace and quickly shoot up the chimney into a light-ish grey whirling cloud tunnel. Soon I am aware of my guardian – a pelican with a pink beak.
>
> Mounting the pelican's back I ride higher with it into the smoke tunnel. In the distance I see a golden mountain rising in the mist...
>
> As we drew closer I see that, built on the top of the mountain, is a magnificent palace made of golden crystal, radiating lime-yellow light. I am told that this is the palace of the phoenix, and I then see that golden bird surmounting the edifice. It seems to be connected with my own power-hawk.
>
> I feel awed and amazed by the beauty of this place, but the regal bird bids me welcome. Then the hawk comes forward and places a piece of golden crystal in my chest. I hold my breath deeply as I receive it, for it is a special gift.
>
> The drum is still sounding but soon Michael asks us to return. However I am still high in the sky and find it very difficult to re-enter the smoke tunnel. When I finally do begin to return the heavens remain golden, and as I travel down into the tunnel I look up to see saint-like figures rimming the tunnel, farewelling me.[24]

The reader may like to compare this description with that given by the author in the chapter on 'Shamanism' in his earlier book on primal religions.[25]

Esoteric magic

Within paganism there is a great emphasis upon ritual rather than on mysticism as found in the main wing of the New Age movement. There is no sharp line between religious ritual and ritual magic. For this reason there are those who have sought to use magic as the means 'to unwrap the secret, inner you and overcome the stress of twentieth-century life'.[26]

People such as Marian Green would not regard this form of magic as being either a religion, nor part of the New Age movement. She would, however, use Aleister Crowley's definition of magic as 'the art of causing changes in conformity with the will of the magician'.[27] This raises one of the major questions concerning magic which is that of its purpose in fulfilling the will of the magician. Marian Green would say that 'the purpose of magic is to help each individual become the most effective, competent and skilled person he or she is capable of being. No one can make you clever, strong or able to work helping or healing magic except yourself.'[28]

The general practice of this form of magic is as follows:

1. Be convinced that magic works, and know what you aim to achieve.
2. Find a place where you will not be disturbed physically or mentally.
3. Gather the equipment you need.
4. Ritually seal the area, 'circle'.
5. State aloud the purpose for which you have gathered.
6. Call upon the name of a particular power or spirit to work.
7. Wait for the power to work. A sign may be given to show the working of the power.
8. Thanks is then given to all who have helped, both visible and invisible.
9. The area is then ritually closed and made safe.
10. Silent meditation may be used to close the ritual.

Magic uses much ritual and symbolism. In fact, magic has

been defined as making a little model of what you desire. The most well known example of this is the voodoo doll in which a wax image is made into which pins are stuck to cause harm to the victim. Most practitioners of ritual magic would decry such harmful practices and claim to use their powers for good. The need for ritual items means that many pagan magazines contain advertisements for incense, robes, candles, herbs, and posters as well as books of ritual magic.

Another important aspect of ritual magic is the need to visualise the desired aim. Meditation may be used as an initial stage in this process, but it is considered necessary to go beyond this to the directing of one's will effectively through the images which have been created.

> ...through experiencing the images creative visualisation can show you, and by learning to see things as they are, you are moving into a greater, virtually infinite world of visions. By recognising what you see as real now, you can create a new future for that scene in which things can be changed for the better. If you have a broken leg, for example, you can see yourself out of plaster, running and jumping with no pain and full strength: you can then work towards that result. See yourself getting stronger, the bones knitting straight and firmly, as quickly as possible. It can happen![29]

A further important aspect of ritual magic is divination. The word 'divination' means communing with the divinity, and thus receiving information that would otherwise be unavailable. There are many types of divination which have been introduced in recent years: tarot cards, I Ching hexagrams, astrological charts, palmistry. Some methods are simple, such as using the nine symbols of divining stones, sometimes called rune stones. The characters on these stones come from the old Scandinavian alphabet. Other methods such as tarot cards are more complex.

Yet another aspect of ritual magic is 'channelling' which is a development of spiritism that has been given a degree of academic respectability. Dr Kathryn Ridall offers courses in channelling, and defines it in the following way:

Channelling is the ability to connect with other beings and other levels of consciousness and express their reality through your body. A channel acts as an intermediary between our physical world and the unseen dimensions of the universe. You could think of a channel as a living transmitter of subtle energies, much like a telephone or a radio station.[30]

The key to channelling is the development of a relationship with a 'guide', or spirit-helper. According to channellers, these may enter into a variety of relations with humans, but they are generally considered to be good and want to help humans especially at this time of world crises. Frequently, guides are regarded as being in a higher state of evolution – humans, but not currently in a body.

Guides on the human path of evolution but between incarnations describe their world as similar to ours in that beings exist in relationships and social groupings. These beings devote themselves to learning and spiritual growth in a much more conscious way than we generally do. The biggest difference between their world and ours is that theirs does not have dense materiality.[31]

The strange syncretism between Eastern religion and Western spiritism is seen in all these writers. The theory of relativity, *karma*, I Ching, Dragon's Blood, and Jungian psychology all occur within the covers of the same book.

Satanism

As we have already mentioned, neo-paganists are concerned to draw a sharp distinction between themselves and satanists. Analytically one can identify a marked difference. Paganists are returning to pre-Christian primal religions, whilst satanists are adopting an anti-Christian position involving a perversion of Christian rites and beliefs.

'Blessed are the strong, for they shall possess the earth. If a man smite you on one cheek, SMASH him on the other!' This is the inverted gospel from Anton La Vey's *Satanic Bible*. La

Vey, and his followers, invoke Satan not as a supernatural being, but as a symbol of man's self-gratifying ego, which is what they really worship. Their rituals are essentially the reverse of established Christian rituals with inverted crosses, good prayers said backwards, and nude women as an altar in the black mass.

Paganists are usually eager to stress that they do not perform any of the rites and activities of which satanists are accused in the popular press. One paganist writes:

> We do not abuse children...
> We do not sacrifice animals (nor babies)...
> We do not have sex orgies....

Although most paganists would separate themselves from such activities, there is an overlap between the paganists and satanists. However, some paganist groups and magazines are at pains to make it clear that they do not want satanists to join their ranks.

Why has there been the growth of satanism? First, the relativistic nature of secular morality allows individuals to do that which they consider right in their own opinion. Individuals who are therefore unable to achieve status through the acceptable patterns for success, such as academic attainment, turn to the use of methods traditionally frowned upon. In this way satanism may be considered as a reaction against Western society and its establishment order.

Secondly, ritual magic provides a sense of excitement through its exotic nature, and the fact that it has traditionally been condemned as evil generates wider interest. Naked dance, illicit sex, and cruelty all attract adherents.

Finally, the current theological climate to accept other religions as valid alternatives to the Christian tradition, therefore leads naturally to the acceptance of 'witchcraft' as just another religion. Secular governments are confused as to how they should act against the growth of these movements if they do not break any existing laws.

Notes

1. Jencson, Linda. 'Neopaganism and the great mother goddess' *Anthropology Today* Vol 5 No 2, April 1989, pp 2–4.
2. Murray, Margaret. *The Witch Cult in Western Europe* (Oxford University Press: Oxford, 1921).
3. Marwick, Maxwell G. 'Witchcraft' in *Encyclopaedia Britannica*, III (Encyclopaedia Britannica: Chicago, 1981) 15th Edition, Vol 19, p 898.
4. Martello, Leo Louis. *Witchcraft: The Old Religion* (Citadel Press: Secaucas) p 59.
5. Gardner, Gerald B. *Witchcraft Today* (Magickal Childe: New York, 1988) p ii.
6. Gardner, *ibid*, p 16.
7. Adler, Margot. *Drawing Down the Moon* (Beacon Press: Boston, 1986) pp 80–85.
8. Adler, *ibid*, p 488.
9. McSkimming, S. 'Gods of the Celts', in *Dalriada: Pagan Celtic Journal* (Lughnassadh 89), pp 4–5.
10. Pennick, Nigel. *Practical Magic in the Northern Tradition* (Aquarian Press: Wellingborough, 1989).
11. Adler, *op cit*, p 252.
12. Castaneda, Carlos. *The Teachings of Don Juan: A Yaqui Way of Knowledge* (Pocket Books: New York, 1968).
13. Jencson, *op cit*, p 4.
14. Personal correspondence with author.
15. Beechs-Squirrel, Nichola. *Statement of Belief of Pagans Against Nukes* (P.A.N.)
16. Pennick, *op cit*, p 258.
17. Pennick, Nigel and Devereux, Paul. *Lines on the Landscape* (Robert Hale: London, 1989) p 13.
18. Chatwin, Bruce. *The Songlines* (Jonathan Cape: London, 1987).
19. Morphy, Howard. 'Behind the Songlines' *Anthropology Today*, Vol 4, No. 5 (1988) p 19.
20. Adler, *op cit*, p 414.
21. *The Pipes of P.A.N.* Summer 1989, No. 32 p 2.
22. Martello, *op cit*, p 80.
23. Adler, *op cit*, p 469.
24. Drury, Nevill. *The Elements of Shamanism* (Element Books: Shaftesbury, 1989) p ix.

25. Burnett, David. *Unearthly Powers* (MARC: Eastbourne, 1988), pp 175–187.
26. Green, Marian. *Magic for the Aquarian Age* (The Aquarian Press: Wellingborough, 1983), cover.
27. Green, *ibid*, p 20.
28. Green, *ibid*, p 21.
29. Green, *ibid*, p 43.
30. Ridall, Kathryn. *Channeling: How to Reach out to Your Spirit Guides* (Bantam Books: Toronto, 1988) p 1.
31. Ridall, *ibid*, p 53.

PART IV

The Christian World

13

THE BIBLICAL WORLDVIEW

In the previous chapters we have considered five major worldviews and some of the interactions which have occurred amongst them. We have endeavoured to consider the strengths and weaknesses of these worldviews. It is now necessary to turn to the question of which worldview does one follow? Everybody has a worldview, and we all need one. Most people are merely born into one culture with its worldview, and spend their whole life in accordance with that paradigm. The fact that the world is becoming 'a global village' means that people will not be left alone with the single option. The ease of travel and the expansion of mass media are presenting people with options their forefathers never dreamed of. New ideas bring revolutionary possibilities for growth or decay of all societies. The fact that the worldviews we have discussed often contain themes which are directly contradictory to those of other worldviews show that not all can be true. One is left with the question, which worldview is the closest perception of reality?

We have made little comment, so far, concerning the nature of the Christian perspective, and its application to our discussion. This is the subject which we shall seek to address in the last section of this book. In this chapter, we need to examine the relationship between Christianity and culture, and then to ask the question, what is the biblical worldview?

Revelation and culture

Historically, people have tended to think of knowing in two

ways. First, there is the objective knowing of analysis and rational deduction, often regarded in the West as the scientific approach. The second level of knowing is the subjective and intuitive. This tends to be more the mystical experiences common in Eastern religions. It is all too easy to enter a debate as to which of these two levels of knowing is most reliable and leads to the most complete understanding of truth.

Our discussion of worldview in the first chapter has shown that it is not possible for human beings to be totally objective in their ability to know. We have grown up within a particular worldview which by the very nature of worldviews appears to us to be right and valid. How then can we know what actually is reality?

Traditionally two approaches have been followed by theologians and philosophers. The first is the use of rational argument within the realm of the material world. This includes such arguments as the Ontological, Cosmological, Teleological and Moral. Thomas Aquinas, one of the greatest exponents of this approach, realised the limits of natural theology:

> If the only way open to us for the knowledge of God were solely that of the reason, the human race would remain in the blackest shadows of ignorance. For then the knowledge of God, which especially renders men perfect and good, would come to be possessed only by a few, and these few would require a great deal of time in order to reach it.[1]

The limits of natural theology lead to the second way of understanding reality. This has traditionally been known by Christian theologians as 'special revelation' in which God is considered to reveal himself to particular people at particular points of time. This is referred to as special revelation because here God acts 'specially', not merely as he always does. When put into written form such teachings have often become the basis for revealed theology in a holy book such as the Bible or the Qur'an.

The traditional Christian view of revelation is that the Bible is the authoritative revelation of God to humanity. The Bible is understood as the source of truth about God, revealing that he exists, what he is like, and what he has done in relationship to humanity. The question then occurs as to how God may speak within the limits of human cultures.

In reading the Old Testament, one sees a growth and change in the Israelite people. Initially, they are a nomadic, pastoral people as seen with the Patriarchs. In Egypt, they are a slave class within a complex and sophisticated civilisation. Following the conquest of Israel, the Israelites develop a society based on agriculture with an elaborate religious system.

Even within the confines of the New Testament one can detect differences in culture. Jesus makes no reference to the Greek athletic games that provide the apostle Paul with so many sermon illustrations. Luke in his writings takes time to explain the meaning of the Jewish rituals to a readership which would have included many Gentiles.

Western culture is so different from that of biblical times that some critical scholars, such as Bultmann, have dismissed much of the Bible as irrelevant. At the other pole, there are some conservative Christians who are looking for a literalist interpretation of the biblical text. One Christian I knew was causing his bank manager much difficulty by refusing to accept the interest from his money deposited with the bank. This was due to a literalist interpretation of Deuteronomy 23:19, 'Do not charge your brother interest, whether on money or food or anything else that may earn interest.'

It is an error simply to take a biblical injunction out of its cultural context and attempt to reproduce it in our society without reflecting upon its significance. Orthodox Jews, for example, believe it is unlawful to eat meat and milk dishes together on the basis of the command, 'Do not cook a young goat in its mother's milk' (Deut 14:21). The original meaning of this command is made clear by an ancient Ugaritic text of the fourteenth century BC which reveals that this was a Canaanite religious ritual. The cultural form is the act of cooking a young goat in its mother's milk, which to the Israelites of that time would carry the meaning of a Canaanite religious practice.

A study of the biblical text shows that many commands are expressed in culturally relevant forms of that society and age. However, there are some which are more abstract and wider in their cultural application. One example is, 'love your neighbour as you love yourself' (Mt 22:39). This command can be expressed within any culture at any time, but the way in which it manifests itself can vary greatly. Charles Kraft has sought to describe three levels of the extent to which biblical injunctions are abstract in their nature: the deepest level of human universals, then worldview values, and finally the level of specific customs (see Figure 13.1).[2]

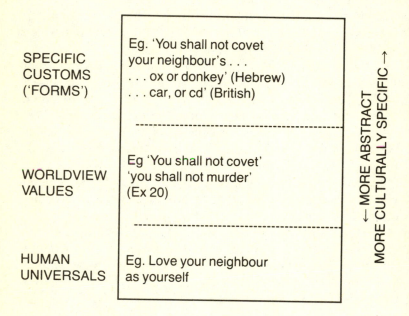

SPECIFIC CUSTOMS ('FORMS')

Eg. 'You shall not covet your neighbour's . . .
. . . ox or donkey' (Hebrew)
. . . car, or cd' (British)

WORLDVIEW VALUES

Eg 'You shall not covet'
'you shall not murder'
(Ex 20)

HUMAN UNIVERSALS

Eg. Love your neighbour as yourself

← MORE ABSTRACT
MORE CULTURALLY SPECIFIC →

Figure 13.1 Biblical injunctions classes from abstract to specific

The universals apply to every person in every culture at all times. These may be regarded as transcultural or even supracultural ideals. The general principles (such as the Ten Commandments) seem, likewise, to apply universally. If these are seen as corresponding with the cultural worldview level (as suggested above) it is with the recognition that values such as these occur in the worldviews of every culture. At the level of specific custom, though, there is a considerable range of diversity expressive of the general principles.[3]

Throughout Scripture we see the transcultural clothed in the specific events taking place in the particular culture. It is therefore necessary to know something of the cultures of those who received that revelation in order to better appreciate the deeper level of meaning. It is this meaning which may then be applied to any culture. Thus, we are unable to speak of just one unique Christian culture, but a multitude of Christianised cultures with a common set of worldview themes.

As we have already seen, a worldview serves many parallel functions to religion within a culture. Thus there is a close relationship between what is generally known as 'Systematic Theology' and worldview. However, worldview is always broader in its scope than is theology, in that it covers issues which are both consciously and unconsciously held by a society. Theology covers only those issues which a society consciously regards as basic assumptions concerning God, man, the cosmos, and the relationship between them.

For this reason in considering the 'biblical worldview', we will attempt to keep the same general set of themes as have been examined in the previous worldviews. The Bible will be regarded as containing a uniform revelation of these themes which are exhibited to varying degrees in different cultures found in the biblical narrative.

The author is aware that he is a product of his own culture, and in reading the Bible he is more conscious of some themes than others. However, in the following analysis the author is attempting to outline the fundamental paradigms presented in the Bible. In doing so he has drawn upon principles accepted by orthodox Christian scholars throughout history.

Biblical worldview themes

The Cosmos

As with all monotheistic religions, the nature and character of deity is of paramount importance in all its worldview themes. How God is understood becomes the foundation to the total worldview, and within the Bible three dominant characteristics of deity may be identified – power, holiness and love.

Before looking at the repercussions of these characteristics it is necessary to state that throughout the Bible, God is regarded as being beyond human comprehension, and he may only be in part understood. Thus, qualities and descriptions of God are limited by the human intellect. Our God is always too small because as created beings we are unable to fully appreciate the nature of the Creator. This is especially seen in the concept of the Trinity which may be regarded as a 'paradigm' for understanding the personhood of God. This model seeks to bring two important truths together: the oneness of God, and the plurality in the Godhead.

The Islamic worldview is monotheistic like the biblical worldview, but it stresses the oneness of God, and rejects any concept of 'Trinity' as blasphemous. The emphasis upon this singular unity makes for a more understandable concept of God, but in so doing imposes a simplification which fails to provide any philosophical answer to the origin of love and communication. Thus, within Islam it is impossible to speak of God loving us because he is transcendent and self-sufficient. The concept of the Trinity, on the other hand, does provide a philosophical answer in that before creation, the three centres of personhood within the Deity were able to love and communicate.

As with Islam, there is a clear distinction between the Creator God, and his creation. Although God is immanent, and everywhere, he is different from his creation; he is 'other'; he is transcendent. The root meaning of the word holiness within the Bible is 'separation' or 'cutting off'. He created the external universe, not as an extension of his own essences as in the Hindu worldview, but out of nothing.

The created order consists of both material ('seen'), and immaterial ('unseen') elements. The material world is that of which mankind is commonly aware, whilst the unseen world is one of spiritual beings. The Bible portrays some interaction between these two aspects of creation. Although the universe is orderly, and follows physical laws which may be studied by man, the universe is not a closed system subject exclusively to cause and effect. As Francis Schaeffer has written, 'God is not a slave to the cause-and-effect world he has created, but is able to act into the cause-and-effect flow of history.'[4] John Wimber argues that our expectations are affected by our worldview.[5] Thus, if we have a concept of God who is outside the universe of cause-and-effect, there will be no way he can work in creation, and so miracles are impossible.

God's creation is portrayed as being essentially good as would be expected of the creation of a good and perfect Creator. However, it was from within the 'unseen' creation that evil emerged, and this eventually led to the fall of humanity and thus of creation as a whole. Two kingdoms are at war. A spiritual battle is going on, a clash which permeates the entire range of human activities.

The Self

The Bible makes a fundamental proposition about the nature of human beings by describing us as being made in the image of God (Gen 1:26–27). This means that man is distinct from the rest of creation, and not merely a highly developed animal. It also means that human beings possess personality because God is personal, and are able to love because God is love. Man is self-conscious, intelligent, creative, and possesses self-determination. One of the problems that the secular worldview faces is how to explain personality. If human beings are made in the image of God they therefore have personality because God is personal. Man is not a machine as the secular worldview must conclude.

Human beings can act into the cause-and-effect world in a

creative way. The world is not an illusion, but a habitat for man in which God has placed him to utilise the resources in a creative and responsible manner. The Bible gives mankind a role as guardian of planet earth as shown in the first command given to Adam (Gen 2:15).

An individual is a total entity consisting of a material body, and also an immaterial part. However, it must be admitted that the church has often been over-influenced by the Greek philosophy of the soul being entombed within the body. Thus, soul and body have often been conceived of as two distinct and separate elements. The Hebrews, on the other hand, believed that at creation humans became living 'souls', and not 'souls' in bodies. 'The Lord God formed the man from the dust of the ground and breathed into his nostrils the breath of life, and the man became a living being' (Gen 2:7). The material and immaterial entities only divide at death. Thus, concepts such as 'soul-loss', 'witchcraft', and the reality of dream activity as found in primal religions, and the New Age movement are not considered to be realities in themselves within a biblical worldview.

Man is a moral being, able to make judgements about what is right and wrong. He has a degree of freedom to choose to the will of God or not. Man rebelled against his Creator, and each person now has a bias towards sin rather than righteousness. Mankind is no longer as it was when first created. Moral disobedience led to a radical change of the whole created order. Man is unable to achieve the perfection of God, although he is not totally evil. This has led to a distortion in man's comprehension of God, the created universe, and also himself.

God is holy, and as such must judge and punish that which is not perfect. At death, therefore, men are judged by God, and are transformed to enter into either an existence with God or forever separated from him. These existences are generally know as 'Heaven' or 'Hell'. Such a judgement and division is not known in the primal worldview where the after-life reflects the contemporary social life.

Knowing

Because man is created in the 'image' of God he has the ability to think and reason. This allows humans to make meaningful scientific experiments, and to 'think the thoughts of God after Him'. Rational thought is possible because mankind has been created in the 'image' of the Creator, and placed within a creation subject to the laws of cause-and-effect. People can therefore discover knowledge about the creation, and so manipulate it in ways they think best. This is what would be expected if mankind was placed in the world 'to work it and take care of it' (Gen 2:15). It is like a father giving his child some modelling clay, and asking the child to create something with the clay.

Even though God is infinite and man finite, God can and does communicate with people. God is so beyond the comprehension of man that this revelation is always limited. God could have remained 'hidden' from man, but it is God's desire to be known and to love. It was God therefore who took the initiative in revealing knowledge about himself. Because human beings can only communicate by cultural forms, he has revealed his truth through cultural terms which were meaningful to the recipients, and it is these revelations which have been written down in Scripture. Thus, as we have already mentioned, the revelation is expressed in the forms of the culture of that particular age and society.

Biblical epistemology is not limited to rational human thought, but recognises the possibility of divine communication. Revelation does not eliminate human reason, but blends into a fuller understanding of reality. Christians must apply their minds to gain a fuller appreciation of the divine revelation recognising all the time that they will never fully understand the mystery of godliness. As the apostle Paul wrote, 'Now we see but a poor reflection as in a mirror; then we shall see face to face. Now I know in part; then I shall know fully, even as I am fully known.' (1 Cor 13:12).

Community

A major biblical theme concerning the nature of human beings is that we all come from one initial parentage. It implies that there is no inherent superiority of one race over another. Individuals are not on some evolutionary scale in which some have progressed further than others.

Human beings are gregarious with a need for social relations and companionship. The Bible continually speaks not only of the importance of the family, but also of the individual's responsibility to the wider community. Within the Old Testament the main community is that of the people of Israel who are often called, in Greek translation, the *ekklesia*. In the New Testament, the concept is given a fuller meaning as seen in the writings of the apostle Paul about the nature of the church. The church is portrayed not merely as a collection of individuals, but as an inter-related organism – a body. As Robert Banks has written following a study of Paul's ideas of community, 'This means that the *"ekklesia"* is not merely a human association, a gathering of like-minded individuals for a religious purpose, but a divinely-created affair.'[6]

The concept of community in the Bible does not take away the importance of the individual. Because each person is made in the 'image' of the Creator, every human being has intrinsic value. Jesus uses the parable of the lost sheep, the lost coin, and the lost son (Luke 15) which illustrate the value of the one amongst the many. Hinduism places little value on the one life, because there are many future lives resulting from endless reincarnations. What does it matter if one beggar dies in the street if he may be reincarnated into a better state? What about the little girl who dies of neglect? She may be reborn as a boy!

If the Hindu worldview neglects the value of one life, the secular worldview goes to the other extreme. Here the value of the individual is so emphasised that social responsibilities are lost in individualism. Western society therefore is suffering from a sense of loneliness in a crowded world, and seeking for community. Perhaps this is the basis of transpersonal psychology, and the desire of the Western witch to link together in the mystical community of the coven.

Human beings are of equal value, although there is a relativism with regards to their abilities. There are 'male' and 'female' aspects to humanity necessary for procreation and companionship. There is an equality of status between the sexes, whilst maintaining a difference in roles.

Time

As with the secular worldview the Bible has a progressive view of time. Time is conceived as stretching backwards, not to infinity, but to the time God created, and forward to the fulfilment of his creation. Time is therefore seen as moving forward meaningfully and purposefully because the Creator has an objective for his creation. This gives a sense of optimism revealed in the Bible in the concept of 'hope'.

Because of God's involvement in space and time, he not only reveals himself in time, but influences the actual events. This is especially seen in the history of the Jewish people which becomes part of the revelation of God to mankind. 'History is the divine purposes of God in concrete form,'[7] writes James Sire.

The most important aspect of the biblical worldview of time is that God entered into time and space in a human form. He did this both to reveal himself more fully, and to achieve his purposes for his creation. The incarnation is the perfect response to the love of God and the justice of God. Here is the answer to the question of what is wrong with the world, and the hope for redemption.

The biblical worldview is a progressive, forward-looking view of time. Time (history) is not reversible, nor repeatable. Hence a person only has one life, and should live that life meaningfully in the light of God's purpose for creation. Mankind has the creative ability to explore and responsibly to utilise the resources made available to him by the Creator. The present world will finally be ended by judgement and then there will be the commencement of a new age.

The secular worldview places great value on time which

results in a great consciousness of measuring time with the associated fear of wasting time. The Bible gives the impression that time is the opportunity for people to fulfil God's will or alternatively rebel against him.

Value

Biblical ethics are not arbitrary, but based upon the absolute nature of the Creator. God is good, and expresses this in the moral principles he has revealed to mankind. Ethical values are absolute. God is the moral standard by which all moral judgements are measured. There is therefore absolute truth, grounded in the Creator, and not manufactured in a relative creation.

The moral standards have been revealed in two primary ways. First, through the human conscience which gives every individual an indwelt sense of right and wrong. The Fall may have affected man's sensitivity to sin, and his cultural analysis of sin, but all people have such an awareness. Secondly, God has expressed his moral standards through the Bible. Although these are based on an absolute, they are expressed in culturally relevant ways. For example, the command not to steal will show itself in various ways depending upon the understanding of ownership within the particular culture. In some cultures, people 'own' their name, and for someone to give the same name to their child is regarded as theft.

Man cannot reach God's standard through his own efforts. All would be punished at the final judgement if God, in the person of Jesus Christ, had not intervened in space and time. Acceptance by God is achieved through personal trust in the life and work of Christ (Rom 5:7–8). A person placing their trust in Christ becomes a member of a new community, the church, through the ministry of God the Holy Spirit.

This is most clearly illustrated in the Bible through the imagery of the kingdom of God. Mankind was not created to live under a legalistic, totalitarian rule, nor under a state of total freedom with no guidelines except those of subjective feelings.

Mankind was created to live in the kingdom of God which would provide a perfect blend of control with freedom, and freedom with control.

Conclusion

Mark Cosgrove, a Professor of Psychology in the States, concludes after a study of modern psychological worldviews: 'I feel that Christian theism offers the most defensible worldview available to psychology. It fits our data and experience. It is broad enough to explain all the data on man, and yet it is detailed enough to be tested.'[8]

Rev Michael Green writes similarly: 'It (Christianity) provides us with the most credible account of the Universe and man's place in it, with the motive and dynamic for serving our fellow men, with the ability to face the harshest situations with realism, and with a message of urgent relevance to the many who suspect Christians of escapism, but are themselves running away from truth.'[9]

It is easy to call Cosgrove and Green, who are committed Christians, ethnocentric. However, that argument would apply to any one of us as we all hold to one worldview or another. Our cultural heritage limits us in our understanding and expression of truth, but a reasonable analysis of various worldviews shows the undoubted strength of the biblical worldview in meeting the five major functions discussed in the second chapter. I can only add my own appraisal that the biblical worldview, if properly understood and applied, meets every criteria for a meaningful and satisfying worldview.

Notes

1. Evans, C. Stephen. *Philosophy of Religion* (IVP: Leicester, 1985).
2. Kraft, Charles H. *Christianity in Culture* (Orbis Books: Maryknoll, 1979) p 142.
3. Kraft, *ibid*, p 141.

4. Schaeffer, Francis A. *The Church Before the Watching World* (IVP: Leicester, 1972) pp 13–14.
5. Wimber, John. *Power Evangelism* (Hodder & Stoughton: London, 1985) p 93.
6. Banks, Robert. *Paul's Idea of Community* (Paternoster Press: Exeter, 1980) p 37.
7. Sire, James W. *The Universe Next Door* (IVP: Leicester, 1977) p 8.
8. Cosgrove, Mark P. *Psychology Gone Awry* (IVP: Leicester, 1979) p 137.
9. Green, Michael. *Runaway World* (IVP: Leicester, 1968) pp 7–8.

14

TRANSFORMING WORLDVIEWS

In the previous chapter we saw how the Bible reveals particular worldview themes. For the Christian, the argument must be as follows. These themes have been revealed by the Ultimate Creator. This means that they are absolute and should therefore be regarded as an ideal for any human culture.

We have already seen that common worldview themes do not necessarily mean that there will be a universality of cultural forms. For example, the Bible stipulates the requirement for individuals to be modestly dressed. However, this requirement will express itself in different ways in different cultures. One society may take modesty to imply that women should be covered from head to foot when in public, whilst another may see this injunction as requiring the covering of only a certain few parts of the body. Both cultures will be convinced that they are fulfilling the command for modesty whilst the other culture is somewhat deviant. The culture requiring the greater degree of covering will regard the second as being immodest by allowing such a degree of physical exposure. The second culture will regard the former as being over legalistic, and even domineering of the female sex. The two cultures may therefore hold to the same proposition for modesty, but will express it in two totally different ways.

An analysis of a particular cultural form can be discussed with relative ease, but what of the matter of a total set of worldview themes which conflict with those of the Bible? We need now to examine further the principles of worldview change. We need to ask the question as to how cultures are

222 / *The Christian World*

transformed and how may the biblical worldview themes become assimilated into a culture? Can a society change to become Christian and yet still retain its own characteristic cultural identity?

It is first useful to consider the transformation of an individual within a culture – the process generally called conversion by most Christians. From this one can move on to consider the wider issues of the transformation of whole societies.

Conversion – a paradigm shift

At university, where I was studying science, I held strongly to a materialistic philosophy. I assumed that all that existed was that which I could study and measure. I rejected any notion of an unseen spiritual dimension to life. When I discussed religious issues with Christians, they would argue from the premise that God existed, and I from the premise that he did not exist. It did not matter if we spoke about the correctness, or otherwise of the theory of evolution, or the merits for or against sexual promiscuity, the outcome was always conflicting views. The problem was that we were starting from fundamentally different assumptions about the nature of reality. The Christians had one paradigm and I another, and a person's starting point will always determine his ending point.

With time I began to see that a materialistic philosophy failed to answer many of the important questions. 'What is the purpose of life?' 'Why am I here having a consciousness of existence?' It is at these points that the secular worldview is at its weakest. It tends to disregard such questions and point people to the benefits of material prosperity. It was in the 1960s, when people had 'never had it so good', that many young people began to look for other answers. I was amongst that generation seeking new answers which would require a new worldview. Some moved towards a Marxist perspective which led to the students' riots which affected Europe during 1968. Others started to follow the lead of the Beatles and explore Eastern religions. Some, including myself, found an answer in the Christian gospel.

For myself the change occurred in the basic assumptions which I held. The failure of the secular worldview led me to re-examine its assumptions, and finally to change my allegiance from a materialistic to a theistic philosophy. To hold to the paradigm that the spiritual world does not exist leads to meaninglessness, and so I adopted a new paradigm which was that there is reality beyond the material world. One of the most helpful books to me as a young Christian was C.S. Lewis' book, *The Screwtape Letters*.[1] This is a series of letters written by a senior devil to a junior devil seeking to influence and ultimately destroy a person's life. C.S. Lewis opened up the 'closed universe' of materialistic philosophy and showed how a fuller, more satisfactory explanation of human life can be obtained by theistic assumptions. From my own perspective I was aware of a change in my way of thinking. However, I realised that beyond this was the intervention of God in my life to bring about this very change which I was experiencing.

I have taken the liberty of such an extended personal narrative in order to clarify what I mean when I speak of conversion being a 'paradigm shift'. For me the shift occurred in a matter of just a few days, and one can find similar cases within the Bible. The apostle Paul is perhaps the most obvious case (Acts 9). Here was a man who was fanatically committed to the Pharisaic tradition with all its legalism, suddenly transformed. However, not all people have such a radical change, and yet they may become equally committed to their new beliefs. The apostles, for example, seemed to take a long time before they understood even who Jesus was.

Although one cannot define a single pattern for conversion, it is possible to identify a common concept. The Greek word which is so often used of conversion is *metanoia*, a word which means to change, or turn. *Metanoia* comes from two roots 'meta' meaning 'after', implying change, and 'nous' meaning 'the mind'. *Metanoia*, according to Vine, is 'after-thought, change of mind, repentance'.[2] It is notable that the Bible does not give any set of outward forms which should occur during this process. However, it is possible to identify certain characteristics of the biblical concept of conversion.

First, God starts where people are. In the Old Testament, somewhere about 2,000 BC, God called Abram to leave his people and his home and go to a new land (Gen 12:1–3). Through the Old Testament prophets, God continually sought to call Israel to return to him. In the New Testament, Jesus calls to the fishermen of Galilee 'follow me'. Here are different people, at different times, and part of different cultures, and yet God starts where they are through the work of His Spirit in their lives.

Secondly, conversion implies a conscious change of allegiance to God. As was described in the first chapter, all worldviews require a degree of allegiance beyond that which can be clearly proven. To state categorically that God does not exist requires as much faith as to say that God does exist. It is only as one seeks to cope with life in accordance with a particular paradigm that it is possible to see how successful it is. The Bible speaks of this as a faith commitment. 'Now faith is being sure of what we hope for and certain of what we do not see' (Heb 11:1).

Thirdly, the biblical understanding of conversion is one which brings about a relationship with God. The paradigm shift is not merely a change to a new philosophy, but to a relationship with a person. This is important as the process is not an intellectual acceptance of some objective assumptions or philosophy, but an introduction to a person. I could ask you if you know a friend of mine. You may answer, that you know of him, but you have not met him. There is a world of difference between knowing of somebody and knowing them as a close friend. It is the establishment of a new relationship which is implied when Jesus speaks of God as being 'Abba', Father.

Fourthly, the paradigm shift becomes a process as the person grows in the grace and knowledge of the Lord. Under the ministry of the Holy Spirit in the life of the person his, or her, character is steadily transformed. The conscience comes more into alignment with the moral truth revealed by God, and the person's behaviour is likewise changed. A process of selection occurs in which the person has to make decisions as to what behaviour and customs of his society are still acceptable for a Christian. The outcome is the establishment of new sets of attitudes and habits.

Fifthly, the work of God's Spirit in an individual's life is not limited to the intellect. If the biblical paradigm that a person is a total being, and not merely a 'soul-in-body' is true, then the transformation should touch every part of the person. This will include the mind, the emotions, the conscience, and the body. One would therefore expect the 'warmed heart' experience of Wesley, and the subjective experience known by many Christians during the history of the church.

Finally, conversion must be worked out in community. The Christian becomes part of a new family, a community of redeemed people with the same heavenly Father. Christians need other Christians with whom to relate and to be assured of the direction and nature of their spiritual growth. This need constitutes one of the reasons for the institution of local churches. As such, Christians become a movement for social transformation.

Christians are often in danger of judging the reality of another's conversion by assessing whether the person is following the established set of behaviour patterns characteristic of a Christian of that culture. In Figure 14.1, it would be equivalent to the circle which Glasser calls a 'bounded set'.[3] A more realistic model would be based on whether people are moving to more Christ-like attitudes and behaviour within their culture, or not. A line could then be drawn around the set moving to Christ, and those moving from him.

When conversion occurs within one culture, the person may take many of their cultural guidelines from other Christians within the society. When the Christian witness comes from a person of another culture (a cross-cultural missionary) it is difficult for the person to easily assess what is essential to Christianity and what is merely part of the missionary's own culture.

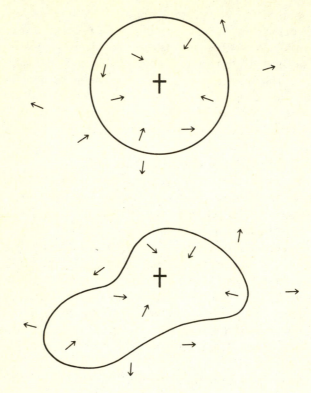

Figure 14.1
Christian commitment based upon behaviour or process.

The missionary has too often tried to see the young convert following his example with the result that the convert becomes extracted out of his own culture into the missionary culture. Kraft has suggested the diagram shown in Figure 14.2 which illustrates this process.[4]

What can happen too easily is that 'Christian conversion' becomes synonymous with 'cultural conversion'. This was the issue which led to the Council of Jerusalem (Acts 15) in the early church.[5] The Judaising Christians were insistent that Gentile Christians should be circumcised and accept Hebrew culture. However, the council finally concluded that Gentiles

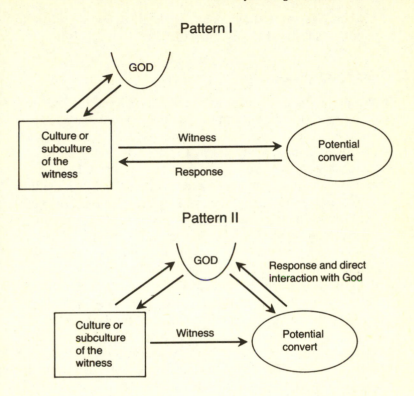

Figure 14.2 Two patterns of conversion to Christianity.

were not required to become Jews as a means to becoming Christians. Gentiles were free to respond to the gospel on the basis of faith in accordance with Gentile cultural forms. Converts should be free to respond and directly interact with God. A cultural transformation will undoubtedly occur, but it will be one from within their own culture rather than a conversion to another foreign culture.

A correct understanding of Christian conversion may avoid difficulties such as that which occurred in Bangladesh. A group of people who had shown interest in the gospel finally responded, 'We like your Christ, but we don't want to become

Christians.' By this they meant that they did not want to become Westerners because they liked their own culture.[6]

Transforming worldviews

In the preceding section we have been looking at the transformation of individuals, but it must be remembered that each person is a member of a particular community. Christians therefore have a dual identity. They are firstly identified with Christ. As Paul expresses this truth in Galatians 2:20, 'I have been crucified with Christ and I no longer live, but Christ lives within me.' Secondly, Christians have an identity with their own cultures. God wants to participate with his people to bring about a refining and purification of their cultures. The well known illustrations of Christians being 'salt' and 'light' reveal this fact. This dual identity often causes a tension for Christians as they seek to live a godly life in the midst of their own societies.

How may the Christian relate to his culture in a meaningful way? The model of Christ is one of the most fundamental to follow — be incarnate! The second person of the Trinity became incarnate as a first-century Jewish male. He took the role of a Jewish rabbi in order to proclaim his message. Even so, he never lost his original identity with the Father.

What principles can be identified for bringing about Christian transformation of worldviews?

First, Christians must be convinced of the essential nature of the worldview themes revealed within the Bible. The problem is that we each read the Bible in terms of our own worldview, or, to use the illustration used at the outset, we each read the Bible wearing our own cultural spectacles. We therefore tend to deal with the text in one of three ways:

a) Those themes which agree with our original worldview are readily accepted as correct and obvious.

b) Those themes which appear to be somewhat different are explained in terms of our contemporary worldview.

c) There are those themes which we tend to neglect altogether because they are not important within our own culture. It may be said that we are culturally 'blind' to these components, and often it is only through interaction with Christians from other cultural traditions that we are able to gain a fuller perspective of the biblical revelation.

Christians must seek to interact with the biblical text from the perspective of their own culture.

Secondly, Christian transformation of a culture must be primarily concerned with changing the worldview themes of that culture. As we have shown constantly, worldview is at the centre of culture, and if this is changed then outward behaviour will change. This is parallel to the views presented on conversion as being a paradigm shift. Once the internal shift has occurred the person's attitudes and behaviour will change.

An important example of a transformation of a worldview theme is found in Jesus' teaching on the concept of community. In answer to the question, 'Who is my neighbour?' Jesus went on to tell the story of the Good Samaritan. Often the significance of the story is lost to the Westerner because we do not appreciate the deep animosity between the Jews and the Samaritans. A Jew wanting to travel from Judea in the south to Galilee in the north had to travel through Samaria by the most direct route. For this reason a good Jew would take a sixty-mile detour around Samaria, and that was on foot. What Jesus was clearly saying to the Jews was that your neighbour is not just the persons who live in your immediate area, nor even fellow Jews, but all people on the face of the earth.

Thirdly, within every culture there are a few key themes which are of paramount importance. An important theme within any worldview is the concept of the nature of deity because it lays an important foundation which has repercussions for other themes. We see Paul speaking to the people of Athens using just this sort of approach, Acts 17:16–34. He commences with their concept of an unknown god, and from this point goes on to present a biblical concept of the nature of the Supreme Creator.

Changes within such key themes have a ripple effect throughout the whole of the culture. Many primal societies know of a Creator God, but he is distant and unconcerned about their personal situations. When they come to know him as a loving God who is concerned about them, this affects their own attitudes to other people. Husbands will love their wives because God loves them. 'Husbands, love your wives, just as Christ loved the church and gave himself up for her' (Eph 5:25).

An interesting example of this change is to be found amongst the Dani people of Irian Jaya. Traditionally, the Dani men lived together in the men's house whilst the wives lived separately with the children. The concept of men loving their wives was little known and a woman was mostly regarded as a possession. Dani men rarely mentioned their wives because they liked to impress others as being free and single.

John Dekker, who worked as a missionary amongst them, recounts,

Christian men began taking only one wife, and loving her. They talked to their wives with growing respect and cared for them when they were sick. Many good marriages grew out of the Dani spiritual awakening.... Instead of the husbands staying in the men's house they wanted to live with their wives. Then they could pray together and have family worship.[7]

Although this transformation resulted in many benefits for the Dani, and was appreciated by them, this was not without difficulties. John Dekker continues, 'But soon the wives became pregnant. Often they were still nursing a baby, and they would lose their milk. With no milk substitute available, this was a problem. Lacking birth control methods other than abstinence, the Dani Christian husbands moved back into the men's house.'

Fourthly, there are many good and useful things which are not found in the Bible. God has given to mankind the creative abilities to explore and use the potentials of his creation. These good things will be discovered by people of different cultures and religions. Thus, something which is good may be found bound up with a mixture of other items some of which may even be evil.

Christians have traditionally followed two viewpoints concerning these good things. Some, because of the evil connections with these good things, have refused to have any association with them. Take, for example, the question of whether Christians should practise yoga. Yoga, as we have seen, is intimately connected with Hindu philosophy. Those holding to this view would have nothing whatsoever to do with yoga, and possibly regard it as demonic.

On the other hand, there are those Christians who would argue that it is possible to extract the good from out of the evil context. Returning to our example of whether Christians should practise yoga, they would argue that there is that which is good in yoga, such as the development of proper breathing, and posture. Christians should therefore claim these good things from within yoga, and use them for the purposes of God.

J.H. Bavinck writes:

> We would, therefore prefer to use the term *possessio*, to take possession. The Christian life does not accommodate or adapt to heathen forms of life, but it takes the latter in possession and thereby makes them new.... The Christian life takes them in hand and turns them in an entirely different direction; they acquire an entirely different content.[8]

This approach would argue that the apostle John tore the 'Logos' concept from out of Greek mythology, and imbued it with new biblical meaning.

Charles Kraft prefers the word 'transformation' rather than *possessio* because it tends to convey the idea of something working from within, rather than from outside as capture.[9] This would indeed come closer to the biblical idea of yeast transforming the dough.

What can be transformed (possessed) from the traditional

African worldview? One thing may be the concept of 'the living dead'. Secularised Christians see death as merely the end of an individual's existence. Christians need to recognise that there is a joy even in death because the person is alive in God and will one day be raised from the dead in a physical resurrection. When C.T. Studd died in the forests of Zaire, the Africans buried his body with shouts of joy, because he had taught them that he was going to be with the Father, and that was far better.

However, there were many aspects of ancestor concepts which we cannot accept. We do not pray for the dead in order to change their state as some Roman Catholics would claim. We do not seek to communicate with the dead, and we do not believe that the dead influence the living.

Fifthly, as we have implied there are not only those things which may be transformed, but there are those things which must be rejected. The missionary coming into a culture from the outside must be careful in his attitudes. So often missionaries have taken the role of moral policemen enforcing a Western moral code upon the Christian converts. 'Drinking is evil; polygamy is evil; chewing cola-nut is evil; smoking is evil....' All these things may be unhelpful, but they are not necessarily the primary issues of concern for the converts' Christian commitment.

There will be those things which the local people will recognise as being crunch issues because they signify their allegiance to Christ. In the Old Testament, the people of Israel were condemned for going to the high places and having sexual relations with the 'sacred prostitutes'. This was part of their idolatrous worship of Baal, and continually condemned by the prophets as such. The local people recognised such practices as indicative that the person was worshipping Baal and not Yahweh. When a person became a true follower of Yahweh this practice had to end. Likewise, in all cultures today there are such crunch issues.

Many Chinese Christians have had to struggle over the issue of making offerings to the family ancestors. The Christian knows that to the non-Christian members of his family these offerings are perceived as worship. Even though it causes much pain and suffering they realise that as Christians they must not take part in such family rituals. In the light of this issue, other issues become small because all know that it is this one which marks for both the Christian and their family the fact that they are true and sincere followers of Jesus Christ.

Daniel was very well instructed in the philosophy and culture of Babylon (Dan 1:20), but he recognised that there was a line beyond which he could not go. For Daniel this related to the issue of eating meat cooked with the blood still in it which was the traditional Babylonian way. This clashed with the Israelite dietary laws, and would cause Daniel to become defiled (Dan 1:8). Later in his life Daniel would not deny his God even in the light of the king's decree to worship no God but the king (Dan 6:10). Within every culture there will be a line beyond which the sincere believer will not be able to cross with integrity. It may vary from one culture to another as to what is the crunch issue, and it may even be an acceptable thing for Christians in one culture but not in another. Each believer must recognise what is the line for himself, and walk in obedience with his God.

Finally, we must understand that societies vary in their openness to change. A society which regards itself as being successful and is confident in its own beliefs is unlikely to show receptivity towards new ideas. The European peoples of the eighteenth and nineteenth centuries are good examples of this. They took little notice of the local cultures, and assumed that they had nothing to learn and much to impart. However, all societies tend to go through periods of loss of confidence which lead to social disintegration. It is at these times that the society becomes open to new ideas. The Roman world at the time of the first century showed all the signs of such disintegration. As a result many new religions were developing within the Roman Empire alongside the growth of Christianity. It was a time for new ideas, and change.

These periods of social confusion cannot be manufactured by the communicator, but they must be recognised by him. One may say that such opportunities are as a result of the sovereign work of God within the peoples of the world. They are like the time of harvest which comes after the fields have been prepared, and the seed sown. At harvest time the workers must go into the fields to reap the harvest. If they delay, the harvest will either be gathered by others, or will rot in the ground.

With the seeming failure of the secular worldview, where are people turning? They are turning to philosophies, such as the New Age movement, which seem to answer the weaknesses of secularism. Here they can find answers to questions concerning the ecology, mystical experiences, and other non-physical phenomena. One may ask, where is the church in providing such answers?

Accommodation

The problem is to find a way of bridging the great difference between the cultural context of the biblical writers and ours today. For example, let us take the various models of the cosmos presented in the Genesis account.

It is quite clear from the early chapters of Genesis that the writer thought of the universe as being composed of three layers: the earth, which was essentially flat and consisting of water and dry land; the 'firmament', which was pictured as a great dome supporting large masses of water, and to which were fixed the heavenly bodies; and finally the 'deep' under the earth, containing the rest of the waters.

Are Christians bound to accept this three-storey model of the universe irrespective of what modern scientific studies have revealed? Alternatively, may we reject the outer form, recognising that God was needing to communicate to man within the limits of his own culture? Does God accommodate his ultimate truth to the limits of human cultures?

First, we need to see that even within the cultures of the Bible times there is a change of perspective. The concept of 'sheol' came into use as the place of the dead which was located under the earth. By New Testament times the Jews had a much more complex concept of the cosmos with the heavens being multi-storied, and God dwelling at the highest level.

Secondly, when Christianity moved into the Roman world, it was the view of the philosopher Ptolomy that became predominant. The earth was seen as being at the centre of the universe, and the heavenly bodies circled around it. This was the model used throughout the Middle Ages by the church who placed Jerusalem at the navel of the world. The church accommodated its own perspective of the Scriptures in terms of the accepted paradigm of the cosmos. God was seen as the one who placed 'the rich man in his castle, and the poor man at his gate'. It appears ironic today, that in 1616, the Roman Church defended this model of Ptolomy against the new discoveries of Galileo.

Thirdly, Galileo discovered, with the aid of his newly developed telescope, that the earth revolves around the sun. As evidence accumulated, Galileo's view prevailed, and as a result another major paradigm shift occurred. This model led to sweeping changes in mankind's understanding of the universe which were soon to be explained by Newtonian mechanics. The birth of modern science had occurred, but along with it came the development of the secular worldview.

After the initial conflict, the church gradually began to come to terms with the new paradigm. Some Christians started to point to the size of the universe as an indication of the majesty of God himself. Other theologians believed that traditional Christianity needed to be reformed in the light of the secular worldview. Miracles came to be questioned, and alternative explanations sought for in the light of modern science. The reality of spirit possession was discounted as being merely the understanding of primitive people. Modern man now considered that such phenomena were actually psychological. Just as before a syncretism occurred between biblical themes and the contemporary worldview as people looked at the Bible through their own 'cultural spectacles'.

John A.T. Robinson's *Honest to God* has sold thousands of copies propounding the view that 'God is Dead', and we must perceive deity as 'the ground of being.'[10] These views are defended on the basis that Christianity must be adjusted to each culture in order for it be credible. Although one would agree the need to make Christianity relevant to a particular culture, if the basic themes of Christianity are removed, Christianity becomes unlike itself. The religion proposed is no longer Christianity, and it becomes anything and everything. It is an unacceptable synthesis. In all expressions of Christianity the same biblical worldview themes must be present in order for it to be Christianity.

Fourthly, the twentieth century has been the period for another paradigm shift, towards Einsteinian mechanics. Although many Christians do not seem to have realised the fact, this has been of as great a significance as that of Galileo. In this case matter is not seen as being solid, but as force-fields and distortions in the space-time continuum.

Why cannot biblical themes accommodate to this contemporary cosmology? The Bible is not a book intended to teach us science. The fact that we can study the universe does not necessarily lead to a legalistic understanding of reality. The so-called scientific laws should not be confused with God's law for creation. Scientific laws are paradigms attempting to account for the order of creation. They are best understood as theoretical approximations of how God orders creation. Newton's law has provided a most useful model for predicting reality, but, as we have seen already, this is limited.

Does all this mean that the Genesis account lacks value and credibility for Western man? Not at all! The Genesis account can be accepted as true and credible if placed in its meaningful context. The account of creation in Genesis 1 is seen from the perspective of a writer actually on earth at that time and in a position to record the developing phases of created life as he experienced them. As Harrison has written: 'What is of primary importance for the Bible student as well as for the scientist is to realise that the Genesis narrative must be interpreted from the standpoint of its anonymous author before pontifications are made as to when it is and is not "scientific"'.[11]

To use another illustration, imagine a video camera set on the face of the earth and recording creation. If one asks, whether the recording is a true account of what occurred, one must answer in the affirmative. Even so, it is only part of the total picture. Another camera placed on the moon would have given a totally different perspective, but it would have been equally true. The problem is that human beings are culturally limited, but God communicates within the limitations of our human cultures.

How relevant are Christians today in communicating to the Western worldview? Has the church become so entrenched in secularism and its ideological and behavioural problems, that it has come to lack the spiritual vitality that many Western people are looking for today? New Agers in their flight from secularism are experimenting with all forms of mystic, spiritual and occultic practices. It is a sad fact that many who are involved in the New Age movement were once church attenders. In their flight from secularism, they have also fled the church. Perhaps it is notable that it is those churches which have exercised spiritual gifts, prayed for the sick, and are believing God for miracles which are the ones which are growing today.

Notes

1. Lewis, C.S. *The Screwtape Letters* (Fontana Books: London, 1963).
2. Vine, W.E. *Expository Dictionary of New Testament Words* (Oliphants Ltd: London, 1940). Vol 3, p 280.
3. Glasser, Arthur. 'An International Perspective' in *Entering the Kingdom* (MARC: Bromley, 1986) Ed. Monica Hill, p 26.
4. Kraft, Charles H. *Christianity in Culture* (Orbis Books: Maryknoll, 1979) p 343.
5. Burnett, David G. *God's Mission: Healing the Nations* (MARC: Bromley, 1986) pp 179–189.
6. Story told by Bruce Nicholls.
7. Dekker, John. *Torches of Joy* (Crossway Books: Westchester, 1987) pp 91–92.

8. Bavinck, J.H. *An Introduction to the Science of Missions* (Presbyterian and Reformed Publishing Co.: Philadelphia, 1960) p 179.
9. Kraft, Charles H. *Christianity in Culture* (Orbis Books: Maryknoll, 1979) p 346.
10. Robinson, John A.T. *Honest to God* (SCM: London, 1963).
11. Harrison, R.K. *Introduction to the Old Testament* (Tyndale Press: London, 1970) p 554.

15

COMMUNICATING WITHIN WORLDVIEWS

The purpose of communication is to bring a receptor to understand a message presented by a communicator in a way that substantially corresponds with the intent of the communicator.[1]

One of the clearest illustrations of how the Christian message may be accommodated to particular worldviews is found in the ministry of the apostle Paul. When one compares the two recorded discourses of Paul at Prisidian Antioch (Acts 13:15–43) and Lystra (Acts 14:15–17) one can see some notable differences. In Antioch, Paul is speaking to a group which was mainly Jewish, whilst in Lystra his audience were people holding a primal worldview.

To the Jews, Paul speaks of them as 'brothers', and identifies with them as a Jew to Jews. On the other hand, amongst the pagan Lystrians he cannot make this association, but he can go to a more fundamental association. We are all part of the same human race, and in cross-cultural evangelism this is always the bottom line for communication.

To the Jews, Paul makes reference to their history referring to people such as Abraham, Samuel, and David. He quotes from their Scriptures as a basis for the message he brings. The people of Lystra had little idea of who Abraham was, or the foreign writings of the Jewish immigrants living amongst them. Paul, therefore, speaks of a God 'who made heaven and earth, the sea and everything in them' (Acts 14:15). He speaks of a God who sends rain for the crops to grow and provide food for

240 / *The Christian World*

them to eat. Here was a supreme Creator God who, Paul showed, was concerned about them.

To the Jews, Paul carries the good news that the promised Son of David has come. 'Through him everyone who believes is justified from everything you could not be justified from by the law of Moses' (Acts 13:39). To the primal society, Paul speaks of a God of all nations who had let them go their own way, but now comes with a message of power and grace.

Paul is presenting the same core message, but he is relating it directly to the cultural context of his hearers. He commences where the people are and expands their comprehension. This is the value of understanding the worldview of a people. It helps us both with regards to our attitude to the people, and to the content of our communication.

The communicator's attitude

The understanding of the culture and worldview of another people will have a great influence on our ability to identify with them.

Because other people may be different from ourselves it is easy to label them as primitive, barbarian, crude, or illogical. Amongst the Eskimos there were two practices which were particularly shocking to Europeans: female infanticide and the suicide of old people.[2] How could parents take their new born baby girls and leave them out in the bitter Arctic cold to die? How could they let their old parents be left behind in the blizzards as the family moves on to new hunting grounds? These practices appear cruel and inhuman, and certainly they are, as even the Eskimo would acknowledge. However, there was a genuine reason for these practices, and an understanding of that reason may help the European to arrive at a new attitude towards these people.

Hunting in the Arctic is a hard and dangerous job which could only be done by the men. Thus, women were essentially food consumers. If there was a shortage of food all would go hungry, and for this reason the old people who were no longer able to hunt or chew the hides were willing to commit suicide. They were willing to give their lives so that the younger people had a better chance of surviving the food shortage. Likewise, if there were too many females as opposed to males in the community, it would be too difficult a task for the men to obtain sufficient food for all. By keeping the ratio of females to males low, it meant that the whole group had a better chance of surviving the harsher conditions.

To follow these practices in areas where there is an abundance of food would be cruel and inhuman, but in the harsh conditions of the Arctic they provided a means by which the society could at least survive. Without these methods the Eskimo people would have died out generations ago.

An understanding of other people leads to a change of attitude. From an ethnocentric perspective one should seek to move to one of empathy. Empathy is the way of comprehending the situation from the perspective of another. It does not mean that one is condoning or condemning, approving or rejecting the other's viewpoint. Empathy is the attitude of appreciating how other people perceive the situation without condemnation. This does not mean rejecting all judgement, but it does mean that there is an appreciation of another's perspective.

Much traditional African art is characterised by images of women with huge elongated breasts, and men with enormous penises. These carvings may easily be disregarded by the Westerner as crude and immoral. These exaggerated sexual organs are meant to represent the fruitfulness of the people in continuing the life of the tribe. A woman represented with huge breasts signifies that she has had many children, and this is a compliment to her fecundity and value to the tribe.

I remember once passing a Hindu holy man sitting cross-legged at the corner of a small south-Indian town. He sat naked with his legs crossed in the lotus position. His body was dirty and covered with white ash, and his matted hair draped down his back. In front of him was a skull, and a basket which seemingly contained a snake. The man was in deep meditation, oblivious to the stares of the new young missionary to India. Why would anyone do such a thing? This was the question which echoed through my mind.

I realised that here was a man who was not dominated by an interest in material things. He had renounced fine clothing, comfort, food, and even personal modesty. These things were only the trappings of *maya*, the world of illusion. He was reaching after the greater goal of *moksha*, release of the self. I struggled within me as to how to share the gospel message with him. Although I came to no simple answer, I did realise that I had taken a major step forward. Not only did I understand the logic of what he was doing, I also empathised with him in his search.

Empathy leads to an identification with the other person. We too are sinners trying to grapple with the perplexing questions of life and meaning. David Hesselgrave has expressed the same thought in these words.

> The missionary in his new situation is a sinner saved by grace. He sinned against God in his own worldview by rejecting the Creator and Redeemer of men. Yet he was captivated by God's truth and love. Such a context makes the missionary a more faithful communicator of the Christian message. Moreover, he is recognised as a person of goodwill who has the best interests of his respondents at heart.[3]

One of the greatest hindrances to the communication of the Christian message to those of the secular worldview has been the communicator himself. Most have failed to understand the rational and apparent success of this worldview. In contrast, Christianity seems out-of-date, and holding to what appears to be a blind faith in some God whose existence cannot be proved by any scientific study. The church seems old fashioned, with rituals born of the Middle Ages, buildings constructed in architectural styles hundreds of years old, and church leaders dressing in ancient costumes. Secularism, on the other hand, stresses that new is best, and as a result the traditional beliefs and practices are rejected.

All too often the Christian communicator has depended

upon well worn clichés, such as 'You must be born again', 'By grace are you saved', whereas these terms have no meaning for the European. Francis Schaeffer has shown the Christian that he should start where the secularist actually finds himself.[4] Starting with an understanding of the worldview themes the meaninglessness and hopelessness of the individual can be exposed. Dissatisfaction with this worldview comes from within the very philosophy itself, but it resides in the heart of the individual himself as emptiness.

The communicator's message

Not only is the attitude of the communicator important, but so also is the way in which the actual message is presented. A standard package such as the 'Four Spiritual Laws' has been widely used with great effect, but it is not universally applicable. All effective communication commences where the people are, and that means from within the context of their contemporary worldview.

Felt-Need

It is not possible to present the entire Christian message on just one occasion. Years of study are required to understand all the historical and theological background to God's plan of redemption, and even then we may only know a part of the total. It is therefore necessary for the communicator to commence with those parts of the story which will be immediately understandable and significant in the lives of the hearers. As we have already seen when speaking to the Jews, Paul commenced with the history of the Jews. This was immediately relevant to them as a people, and allowed the development of the theme to the person of Christ. To the Gentiles, Paul commenced with the God who created the universe and all people.

No worldview totally satisfies the people of a society. The worldview may meet some aspects of cultural need very well, but will fail in other areas. As we have seen, the secular worldview has provided well for the physical needs of humans, but it has failed to answer some basic questions concerning the meaning for living. The primal worldview, on the other hand, has not been so successful in meeting physical needs, and so often it has been the demonstration of the power of God which has transformed societies.[5] This is seen with the case of Paul in Lystra. It is the miraculous healing of the lame man which led to an openness amongst the Lystrian people.

I found that my own testimony of becoming a Christian was of great value in speaking to college students in Africa or Asia, but irrelevant to tribal people. My questioning as to whether God exists seemed laughable to them with their worldview. They are very aware of the spiritual realm, and have no doubt that God, or gods, exist. Their concern was about how God may break into their own situations for healing, deliverance from the demonic, and general physical well-being.

As we have seen, a dominating concept in Hinduism is that of *karma*. It has a Christian parallel in the teaching, 'A man reaps what he sows' (Gal 6:7). In Hinduism, *karma* is a law dominating, not only human beings, but gods and demons. All living creatures seek for liberation (*moksha*), and the bliss of identity with the ultimate. The concept of *karma* may be a useful starting point in the presentation of the gospel. The gospel goes beyond *karma* with the message of forgiveness through the cross of Christ. It is necessary to realise that this process also works in the other direction. Some in the New Age movement have referred to passages such as Galatians 6:7 as evidence that the Bible implies the truth of *karma*.

Adaption of the Message

Not only must the communicator commence with the needs felt by the society, but he, or she must carry out the continual process of adapting the message to the hearers. To the Jews, Paul continually refers to their own history and Scriptures. Whilst, to the Gentiles, Paul speaks about the God who sends rain, and provides food.

The process of communication must work from within the

existing cultural forms for them to be meaningful and relevant for the people. This is most simply described by illustrations from Bible translation. The Greek word *theos*, and the Germanic *guth* conveyed different concepts of deity than that taught in the Bible. These were, however, generic terms rather than names of particular gods, and were imbued by Christians with new meaning. Amongst primal societies many have a notion of a supreme Creator God, and the name of this God has been found to be meaningful and helpful in communicating the Christian concept of God.

God is willing to accept people at the point where they are, with the understanding that they have, and transform those concepts. Charles Kraft has referred to how God is willing to start work within a people's existing intellectual framework of deity in the Old Testament.[6] The commandment to have 'no other gods before me' (Ex 20:3) seems to imply that the early Israelites did believe in the existence of gods other than Yahweh. Jonah seems to have assumed that he could avoid having to follow God's command by running away from God's territory, and presumably into the territory of some other god. These cases seem to illustrate that the early Israelites had a less than ideal understanding of God, but the important issue is that God was willing to accept them as being valid starting points in their understanding of his true nature.

On the other hand, God was not willing to accept those who worshipped Baal. 'Apparently God was (and is) willing to tolerate belief in other gods but not devotion to them.'[7] An allegiance to another god is an unacceptable starting point, and as such demands a change of allegiance before God's process of transformation can begin. This is what Allan Tippett has called 'power encounter'.[8]

Thus, one can see that there are various paradigms of deity which God is willing to accept as starting points in the process of transformation to a fuller perspective of the true nature of God. One may say that it is impossible for any human being to have a total understanding of God because we are limited, and he unlimited. However, through a study of the Bible, and by the ministry of the Holy Spirit one can gain a fuller and truer paradigm of God (see Figure 15.1).

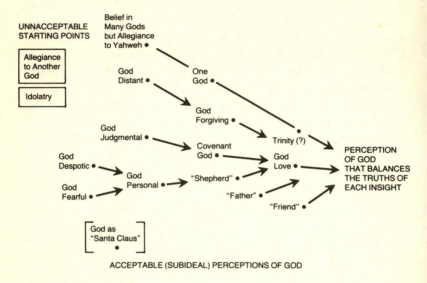

Figure 15.1 Starting-point-plus-process model applied to scriptural perceptions of God's nature. (Kraft 1979)

Bridges for Communication

Worldview provides a storehouse of meaning and illustration. The whole of Jewish culture provided illustrations of God's truth which was widely used by the apostles. The great passage on the Servant of God in Isaiah 53 provided a major bridge for communication for the early church as seen in Acts 8:26–40. Jesus makes reference to 'the sign of the prophet Jonah' (Mt 12:39), 'Moses lifted up the snake in the desert' (Jn 3:14), 'the True Vine' (Jn 15:1), and many other Old Testament illustrations.

Gentile cultures do not contain such a wealth of material which is illustrative of God's revelation, but this does not mean that it is totally absent. Don Richardson in his book *Eternity in their Hearts* has argued that within every culture there are illustrations which are useful and meaningful for the communication of the gospel.[9] This was most dramatically illustrated in his book *Peace Child* in which he uses an analogy from the Sawi culture to communicate the Christian message.

Another interesting example comes from the north of Ghana where many people fear the ancestors, and offer sacrifices to placate them. Frequently the people will say, 'If I become a Christian, the spirits of my ancestors will not be happy with me. They will come and cause me trouble. I am afraid of what they will do to me.'

Dugan Lange has sought to address this issue directly.[10] In the cool of the evening he would sit with the men of the village and talk with them about their ancestors. (M is missionary, G Ghanaian).

M   Do you have a father?

G   Yes, of course I have a father.

M   Let this stone represent your father.
Place a small stone on the ground to represent the person. Stones do have a symbolic relationship in the minds of these people to the ancestors.

M   Did your father have a father?

G   Yes, of course.

M   Let this stone represent your father's father.
(Put a second stone on the floor next to the first.)

M   Did your father's father have a father?

G   Yes, of course.
(Put a third stone on the floor to make a line.)

M   Which of these ancestors has most power?

G   It is the father who brought the son into the world. Therefore the father is always greater.
(Continue the conversation until you have a long line of 20 or 25 stones.)

M   Do you know the name of this ancestor?, pointing to the last stone.)

G   No, I can only remember back about twelve generations.

M   Surely, this ancestor must be very powerful and close to God. God's Word tells us the name of the first man was Adam. If he was the first man then God must have made him. So that makes God his father.
(Place a large stone next to the one representing Adam.)

> M   This stone must be very large to show us the power of God. Out
>   of all our ancestors, which one has the most spiritual power?
> G   Adam. He was the first.
> M   God spoke directly to Adam. But, before we talk more about
>   him, I want to ask you a second question. Who taught your
>   father about sacrifices?
> G   He learned it from his father.
> M   Who taught your father's father about sacrifices?
> G   His father.

Once more the conversation continues until you reach Adam.
This allows one to speak about Adam's sin, and the promise
God made to him that someday a person would be born who
would deliver people from the power of Satan, sin, death and
suffering (Gen 3:15). This would be God's powerful sacrifice to
pay for our sins.

> M   That powerful sacrifice was Jesus, and we have come to bring
>   you the good news about the fulfilment of God's promise to
>   your first ancestor.

This story can be enlarged to cover many aspects of the biblical
story, but the important point to note is that it begins where the
villagers are, and relates to the fears and needs they have.

The communicator's world

It is all too easy to consider that Christian communication is
merely a matter of presenting a worldview which is more satisfactory than the one already held by the receiver. Although,
there is truth in this, it must not be forgotten that if the Christian
believes the biblical account to be the revelation of the absolute
Creator God, it must allow a person to gain a worldview which is
a closer approximation of reality. This will result in some
important repercussions for the life and communication of the
Christian. As we have seen, the purpose of worldview is that it
allows one to cope successfully with one's environment. The
Christian should seek to live with integrity within the foundation of his worldview. A failure to do so makes him to appear a

hypocrite to others, and deficient in his life-style.

Firstly, because the biblical worldview recognises a God who acts in space and time, then one should expect God to be working in and through his people. This may be seen in the local context as miracles, and in a wider context God's superintending of history to accomplish his purposes. Prayer should become a priority issue because within the biblical worldview it is communication with the Creator and the Sustainer of the universe. He should also acknowledge the power of God at work in his own life through the ministry of the Holy Spirit which God promised (Acts 1:8).

Secondly, the biblical worldview also recognises the reality of spiritual beings who are in conflict with the purposes of the Creator. These beings cannot be merely placed in the area of academic discussion, but must be recognised as powerful forces seeking to cause confusion and destruction.

One fundamental area in which confusion can be caused is in our perception of reality. In the first chapter, we spoke of how our conception of reality is limited through our senses, and through our attention. One may add a third, the distortion due to evil. Or as Paul expresses it in 2 Corinthians 4:4, 'The god of this age has blinded the minds of unbelievers, so that they cannot see the light of the gospel of the glory of Christ, who is the image of God.' One must therefore be discerning in what one does and what one accepts as truth. To become involved with some magical ritual may appear harmless fun from the perspective of the secular worldview, but a recognition of such spiritual beings should warn one of the inherent dangers of such practices. There is a great danger in the sample-and-see approach to the various religions and practices on offer in the world today.

Thirdly, the biblical worldview acknowledges salvation for some humans and damnation for others. Although one may argue that the terminology for hell as being a 'lake of fire' is a paradigm, the truth behind it is clear. Hell is an awful place of judgement. We either walk in the light and have eternal life, or walk in the darkness, and experience eternal death. Christians should be motivated in sharing the good news of the kingdom of God with all peoples everywhere.

Culture is a gift to every person from his society. The ideas, values and assumptions which make up a worldview are a precious heritage from previous generations which seeks to enable the individual to cope successfully with their present day environment. Worldviews vary in the degree and areas in which they are able to meet human needs. The Christian must believe that there is a need for the themes divulged within the biblical revelation to be brought within every culture. However, this must not freeze us into one particular culture which we regard as the only Christian culture. The biblical worldview allows a richness of expression in many meaningful forms. The knowledge of contrasting perspectives must shatter the illusions of old boundaries, and encourage the richness of Christianity in many cultural forms.

Marshall McLuhan has written:

> Hitherto most people have accepted their cultures as fate, like climate or vernacular, but our empathic awareness of the exact modes of many cultures is itself a liberation from them as prisons. We can now live, not just amphibiously, in divided and distinguished worlds, but in many worlds and cultures simultaneously. We are no more committed to one culture—to a single ratio among the human senses—any more than to one book or language or technology. Compartmentalising of human potential by single cultures will soon be as absurd as specialism in subject or discipline has become.[11]

The increasing world population, the communications revolution, and growing urbanisation will mean that mankind will no longer be able to exist within isolated cultural, national or racial boundaries. A new world consciousness is emerging which recognises cultural diversity and syncretism.

The church must not be slow in perceiving these trends, but see the opportunities which they provide. Two principles must be adhered to by all Christians:

1) An adherence to biblical principles. We need to read the Bible in terms of both its cultural setting and our own cultural heritage. This will enable us to see the fundamental truths which must be held as immutable. We will need to recognise the essential themes as opposed to the cultural details. These

themes must be present within the goals to which all Christians seek to transform their cultures. This is often highlighted in the formulation of national laws which express biblical foundations.

2) A recognition of a multitude of cultural forms in which the biblical worldview can be manifest. We need to think in terms of the Christianisation of cultures rather than one idealised Christian culture. Every flake of snow has a different crystalline form, but they are all based upon the same structure of the ice crystal. Unity does not mean uniformity, but it does require a commonality of fundamentals.

Knowing another culture may free one from or freeze one to the culture of origin. Can Christians from different cultures reach across those cultural barriers, and take hold of the hand of another and say, 'My brother?' Can we recognise the richness of our own cultural heritages and see these transformed under the enabling of the Holy Spirit?

Notes

1. Kraft, Charles. *Christianity in Culture* (Orbis Books: New York, 1979) p 147.
2. Nida, Eugene. *Customs and Culture* (Harper & Brothers: New York, 1954) p 47.
3. Hesselgrave, David. *Communicating Christ Cross-culturally* (Zondervan: Grand Rapids, 1978) p 134.
4. Schaeffer, Francis. *The God Who is There* (Hodder & Stoughton, London, 1968).
5. Burnett, David G. *Unearthly Powers* (MARC: Eastbourne, 1988).
6. Kraft, *op cit*, pp 243–4.
7. Kraft, *op cit*, p 243.
8. Tippett, Alan R. *God, Man and Church Growth* (Eerdmans: Grand Rapids, 1973) pp 88–91.
9. Richardson, Don. *Eternity in Their Hearts* (Regal Books: Ventura, 1981).
10. Lange, Dugan J. *Ancestors and Sacrifice: Bridges or Barriers to the Gospel* (1989) Unpublished paper.
11. McLuhan, Marshall. *The Gutenberg Galaxy* (University of Toronto Press: Toronto, 1962).

INDEX

Unearthly Powers

by David Burnett

Primal religions pervade every nation: for some they are the foundations of life, for others their influence is unrecognised but crucial.

The term 'primal religions' covers a wide range of the major world religions. They are often scorned by Westerners as being no more than exotic customs, wild dances and primitive sacrifices.

Yet ghosts, possession, the evil-eye and sorcery touch the lives of many people within their folk religion. Even in our secular culture many people turn first of all to the horoscope in their morning paper, and others experiment with spiritism, witchcraft and new religious movements. David Burnett draws on careful research and first-hand experience to explain the worldviews, beliefs and practices of folk religion.

Unearthly Powers challenges us to bring the Gospel, in power and by careful teaching to bear on the world of primal belief.

Dr David Burnett is Principal of the Missionary Orientation Centre at WEC International, and a Fellow of the Royal Anthropological Institute.

MARC
Monarch Publications